SG Productions

I0638479

First Edition 2025

For permission requests, write to:
Sankarsingh Gonsalves Productions
c\o neil@sgproductions.ca

ISBN
Softcover - 978-1-0688832-2-4

For my children Keeghn, Gabriella and Hunter

Never be afraid to think differently and speak openly. Regardless of whether you are right or wrong, you can always learn from controversy; but to surrender to conformity is to betray the very name of our species. Homo Sapiens (Wise Human)

Introduction

A well-written book is like a close friend: providing insights when you're in a quandary; empathy when you are hurting; laughter when you need it, and escape from the mundane. This is such a book. Within these pages, you will find not only stories but solace. You will meet a person whose flaws mirror your own, and whose triumphs may ignite sparks of courage within you. A person who shares profound insights into many of the things we all struggle with – relationships, health, politics, and the human condition. In this book Gonsalves' journeys are not just his—they become ours, reflecting the shared human experience with all its complexity, beauty, and occasional absurdity.

The book is divided into five major topic areas: Observations, Reflections and Lessons Learned; Politics, Policy and Society; Finding Our Common Humanity Amidst Conflict and Division; Challenges in the Education System and Opinion Editorials In Newspapers. In each of these sections Gonsalves explores thematic influences and dives headlong into the thorniest and most problematic areas of the topic.

Books have an uncanny way of showing up when we need them most. Whether you picked this one up deliberately, stumbled across it by accident, or received it as a gift, I believe there's a reason it found its way into your hands. Perhaps it will make you laugh when the world seems too serious. Perhaps it will make you cry when you need permission to feel deeply. Or perhaps it will simply keep you company when the quiet gets too loud.

With its wide range of topics, this book will feel like sitting down with an old friend, the kind you can call at any hour. It won't offer all the answers, but it will ask meaningful questions. It won't avoid the messy parts of life but embrace them—because, after all, that's where the magic happens. Some of the most profound growth comes not in moments of certainty but in moments of uncertainty.

So, here's to getting lost—and maybe even finding something—between these pages. Whether you read it in one sitting or savor it slowly, know that this book will be here whenever you return. Open the cover, turn the page, and let's begin.

Welcome, friend. You're exactly where you need to be.

Brian Sankarsingh

Section 1
OBSERVATIONS, REFLECTIONS, AND LESSONS LEARNED

Summary

Imperfect and cracked, we stumble through the mess, yet every day they rise—because trying, even when flawed, is still an act of courage and determination. There is not even one among us who can lay claim to perfection. Some relentlessly pursue it not realizing that it is our imperfection that makes us who we are.

Finding who we are requires deep and truthful and often painful reflection on our lives, relationships and career. That is when we discover the person we have become; that is when we reveal the person we are. This is not an exercise of self-imposed guilt, loathing or regret, although it can be. Shining a light on our imperfections is always dangerous. But we become better humans if we are strong enough and willing to understand ourselves.

Death of the Centrist

Published by Seeking Veritas on Substack: Dec 08, 2024

A lot of ink has been spilled in recent years dissecting and analyzing polarization in society. As a natural by-product of our inherent tribal nature, we have a tendency to direct our ire towards one end of the ideological spectrum or the other, often embodying the very rhetorical divisiveness we aim to elucidate. Like just about everything else, polarization does not exist in a vacuum, it is the naturally occurring result of the push and pull of the social pendulum. Upon further reflection I have come to believe that there is more to the phenomenon than a sudden adherence to rigid ideological fealty. Our current state of polarization did not come into the world full grown; it was birthed in a bio-psycho-social ecosystem whose genetic code gave it all the predispositions necessary for its existence. And, in keeping with the natural cycle of life, its birth is aptly juxtaposed with the death of the centrist.

On the Right

Donald Trump's success at the ballot box in 2024 was not met with the same shock as his previous success in 2016. There were no pussy hats and mass marches this time around and few were surprised by his win. For one thing he won the election with clear majorities in the electoral college and the popular vote, even more notable was the fact that he cobbled together one of the most diverse coalitions in recent Republican history. However, there is more to the story, I said this back in 2016 and it may just be worth repeating again. To view the initial rise and the resurgence of Trump in a uniquely North American context is myopic because he is hardly a trail blazer, on the contrary his success fits squarely in the middle of the global political bell curve.

For the better part of the last twenty years the global electorate have been shifting to the right. There has been a rapid rise of populist leaders and parties in power across the world since the mid-2000s. The prevalence of populism remains near its 30-year high. Several right-wing populists have achieved significant electoral success in recent years in countries such as Poland, Hungary, Switzerland, Denmark, Austria, Finland, France, Italy, the Netherlands, Norway, Latvia, Sweden and Germany.

Even though some recent populists have been ousted from power such as Brazil's Jair Bolsonaro, Slovenia's Janez Janša, Rodrigo Duterte of the Philippines and Sri Lanka's Gotabaya Rajapaksa, the political landscape is still home to many others like Hungary's Viktor Orban, Narendra Modi in India, Giorgia Meloni in Italy, Netherlands' Geert Wilders, Andrzej Duda of Poland, Recep Tayyip Erdoğan in Turkey and others cut from the same cloth. The far right has steadily ascended across Europe and a Marine Le Pen presidency in France grows ever more likely as French citizens continue to protest against the Macron government.

Populism becomes increasingly attractive to the public when there are real social and economic problems. Immigration and religion are often central to many populist movements but economic factors such as a perceived poor economy, imbalances in international trade, and increased reliance on artificial intelligence contribute to growing alienation among the citizenry, making nationalistic policies appear preferable. Chief among the grievances leading to feelings of disenfranchisement are the perceived impacts of globalization.

Indian economist Arvind Subramanian who coined the term "hyper-globalization" posits that globalization began slowly in the 1970s, accelerated through the 80s and 90s, and exploded into the twenty-first century. On a global level this forty plus year trajectory was generally viewed as positive and beneficial.

As Michael Cox states in his article Understanding the Global Rise of Populism - "The new economic order generated enormous wealth, drew in once previously closed economies, drove up the world's GDP, encouraged real development in countries that had for years been poor, and most important of all in terms of human welfare, helped reduce poverty too".
The interplay of globalization and technological change fundamentally shifted the balance between labour and capital. A globalized economy benefits people in developing countries (the global south as they are more commonly called today), and elites in advanced countries, but as Thomas Piketty argued in his book 'Capital in the Twenty-First Century' it does not do much for the middle class in developed economies. Middle class incomes stagnated, working class jobs moved to

countries with cheaper labour supplies, and local businesses had to contend with a major influx of cheap imported goods. All of this was great for the corporations and the consumers but devastating to the interest of labour and the unions that represented them.

Conservative retrenchment, led by Ronald Reagan and Margaret Thatcher in the 1980s raised doubts about government's competence, and in many ways set the stage for the current rebranding of conservatism. For a long time, conservatives were seen as the party of business and the elites; working class people often aligned with liberal or center-left parties, which championed unions and labour interests. However, as manufacturing gave way to the knowledge economy, left leaning parties increasingly shifted towards supporting globalization and their core constituency morphed from the blue-collar workers to the professional and the highly educated class who benefited from the knowledge economy.

This shift opened the door for center-right and far right parties to capitalize on the growing resentment among nativists and the economically disaffected. It allowed them to grow their base by finding common cause with those who feel like their children would be worse off than previous generations. They could finally move away from the god, guns and sex narratives they had been saddled with, opening the door to address kitchen table issues exacerbated by inflation, by precarious housing and employment, and by mass immigration.

A strong argument can be made that there exists a consistent latent cultural effect in Canada, whereby we exhibit social tendencies that mirror our southern neighbours. This almost predictably puts us on the same trajectory as the United States. Many in Canada would argue that the Conservative Party in Canada is poised to win the next election. Polling currently indicates that the Conservative Party holds a 19-point lead over the Liberal Party and is in a strong position to win a big majority government with the potential for a net gain of nearly 100 seats.

The current Conservative leader also has timing on his side. Electorates predictably yearn for change around the ten-year mark making it increasingly challenging for incumbent leaders to hold on to power at that tipping point.

Term trends for Canadian Prime Ministers over the last forty years supports this assertion. Brian Mulroney's Conservatives governed Canada for nine years from 1984 to 1993, before Jean Chretien's Liberals ousted them and governed for ten years from 1993 to 2003. The pendulum swung back to the Tories with the election of Stephen

Harper who held office for nine years from 2006 to 2015, only to get swept in the 2015 Liberal tidal wave that brought Justin Trudeau to power. - if you're keeping score, that would put him in office for ten years at the time of the next election, and as I have often said, human behaviour is extremely predictable.

Despite positive polling data and trend analysis on his side Conservative Leader Pierre Poilievre's campaign has relied on a "populist lite" messaging strategy, relying heavily on three word catch phrases such as 'Axe the Tax', 'Spike the Hike', 'Build the Homes', 'Stop the Crime' and 'Defund the CBC'.

The unfortunate part of what is being presented to the public is the fact that Poilievre actually has defendable policy positions that could address current Canadian economic woes. He has argued effectively for the contraction of bureaucratic expenditure in housing production. His policy approach favours lower immigration targets tied to housing capacity, as well as faster recognition of foreign qualifications for economic immigrants.

Poilievre's energy policy focuses on maximizing Canada's energy sector; including natural gas exports, which he claims will be a net gain for climate science on a global scale based on providing a better alternative to coal used in Asia. Economically, he envisions business growth including future energy supported opportunities for data centres. A return of Canadian investments for pension plans and the like, most of which is lost to the US presently. He argues for a more fiscally conservative monetary policy to manage runaway inflation and address the cost-of-living challenges that appear to be a top priority for many Canadians.

In an age of information overload, sound bites and social media, the catchy phrases appeal to many who don't want to dig into the policy weeds but diminishes the quality of our discourse. It borrows a page from the populist playbook located right of traditional conservative politics.

On The Left
As the knowledge economy came to dominate social and economic discourse, the left found new constituents and donors within the top quintile of society. This demographic shift had profound influence on policy agenda and party rhetoric. This shift was amplified by major events like the Great Recession, the rise of the Tea Party in the United States, the Occupy Wall Street movement, the killing of George Floyd and the COVID 19 pandemic, as well as the growth of right oriented parties across Europe, like the Alternatives for Germany, the left leaned into social justice activism and identity-

based politics. The shift solidified the allegiance of the knowledge professionals but also began to fracture the relationship with blue collar voters whose concerns seemed to play second fiddle to abstract symbolic priorities of the top quintile.

It is tempting to see recent social justice activism, sometimes pejoratively referred to as 'Being Woke', as a contemporary call to action and a long overdue response to social injustices; many would like to believe that the 'Great Awokening' of the last decade is proof positive that the enlightened among us are blazing a new trail that will lead the oppressed out of the proverbial desert, while allies and advocates usher away the oppressors with chants of "Shame! Shame! Shame!" - Except we've seen this movie before, and it may not end as predictably as one might expect.

"Great Awokenings", sudden onsets of intense concern about prejudice and discrimination have happened at numerous points throughout Western history. One of the earliest references date back to the 1860s during Abraham Lincoln's presidential election when a movement with half-million members called the 'Wide Awakes', campaigned for worker's rights and the abolition of slavery. The word woke itself was employed in similar parlance as contemporary usage in a 1938 blues song by Huddie Ledbetter, his song about "the

Scottsboro Boys, nine black teenagers wrongly accused of rape and sentenced to death, warns of the dangers of a racially prejudiced justice system" and concludes with the lyrics 'best stay woke'. By 1965 the New York Times recognized woke as one of the "hip idioms in black vernacular" and Martin Luther King evoked the metaphor of wokeness, when he called upon his audience to "remain awake through a great revolution". Yet for many contemporaries, the word is more commonly credited to the Black Lives Matter movement founded in 2012, with some citing the 2007 Erykah Badu song 'Master Teacher' as its originating source.

Sociologist Musa al-Gharbi in his book 'We Have Never Been Woke' posits that there have been at least three periods of 'Great Awokenings' in America beginning in the early twentieth century. By his account, prior to the current 'Great Awokening', in all three previous cases strikingly similar social conditions brought about intensified activism. The first was around the time of the Great Depression of the late 1920s and early 1930s. The second in the mid 1960s at the height of the civil rights movement and the Vietnam war and last a smaller awokening in the late 1980s and early 1990s around politically correct speech, proxy wars and emerging globalization.

In all three cases economic downturns and wars created the pretext for a sudden hyper focus on social issues. In all three cases relatively, young adults grew increasingly hostile towards the older generation, the perceived elites, who they considered to be out of touch. In all three cases the disenfranchised middle class aligned their interests with those most marginalized in society and began demanding that the system needed to be overturned.

However, Musa al-Gharbi also argues that people who work in fields like education, entertainment, media, law, human resources etc, who he refers to as 'Symbolic Capitalists', routinely co-opt the issues of the truly marginalized and extract opportunities that satisfies their own interests often with little tangible benefit to the actual poor and marginalized.

Al-Gharib defines Symbolic Capitalists as - "those who possesses a high level of symbolic capital, and exerts control over, and extracts profits from, the means of symbolic (re)production... [and] whose social position is tied to the production, distribution and transformation of symbolic capital"
In essence many on the left have leaned strongly towards identity-based politics emphasizing difference over common cause. Unfortunately, these characteristically cerebral and symbolic interests increasingly appeal to, and resonate with a small, albeit well educated and

relatively affluent segment of the electorate. The ubiquity of social media has driven these issues from academia to popular culture often completely by-passing the very real kitchen table issues that concern the broader public.

"In an American post-election YouGov survey of working-class (non-college) voters for the Progressive Policy Institute, 68 percent of these voters said Democrats have moved too far left, compared to just 47 percent who thought Republicans have moved too far right. It's a fair surmise that working-class sentiment about the Democrats' leftism is heavily driven by the party's embrace of cultural leftist positions across a wide range of issues (immigration, crime, race, gender, etc.) given how unpopular these positions are among those voters."
- Ruy Teixeira - Economic Populism: Opiate of the Democrats

The Liberal Party in Canada has had several policy wins they could campaign on that could address real issues, such as its dental health program, their $4-billion housing accelerator program, and the universal pharmacare program, which 'The Society of Obstetricians and Gynaecologists of Canada' hailed as a "historic achievement" stating "Women across the country will be able to make choices about contraception based on what's best for their lives, not their wallets". Yet more people remember the announcement that all federally regulated employers must provide free menstrual products in all employee washrooms including bathrooms assigned for biological men. Messaging matters and the Liberals are missing opportunities to make their case.

A strong argument can be made that there exists a consistent latent cultural effect in Canada, whereby we exhibit social tendencies that mirror our southern neighbours. This almost predictably puts us on the same trajectory as the United States. Many in Canada would argue that the governing Liberal Party has veered further left compared to its historical roots and in some cases is indistinguishable from the NDP - who campaign significantly further left of traditional Liberals politics.

If the Liberals are borrowing from the Democratic Party's playbook in the US, they may a little late to make the case that there is more to them than virtue signalling.

The Center
Instead of expanding the Overton Window, we have merely created twin windows set diametrically opposed from each other. Both the left and the right have shifted further towards the edges of the ideological spectrum appealing to fewer and fewer people in the main. It makes for great theatre but is unquestionably light on substance.

The rise of the Tea Party and the Occupy Wall Street movement are useful analytical examples that may highlight how the centrists lost standing in our modern political discourse in North America.

The Tea Party has been described as a 2009 right-wing populist movement that rose in the aftermath of the election of American President Barrack Obama, it took its name from the 1773 Boston Tea Party movement of the American Revolution. They boasted that their decentralized approach allowed for greater autonomy and avoided their grassroots movement front being co-opted by traditional political interests.

They did not have a uniform agenda but broadly opposed government oversight, amnesty for illegal immigrants, sought reduction in government spending and opposed tax increases and healthcare reform. Tea Party supporters tended to be more "financially stable than the general population, with 31% reporting family incomes in excess of $75,000 a year; and Tea Party supporters are more highly educated, with 37% reporting college degrees as compared to 25% in the general [American] population".

The movement did not achieve most of their stated goals, but they did significantly disrupt the political landscape. In many ways they brought back the politics of anger and outrage establishing the foundation of American right-wing populism. The politicians who aligned themselves with the movement did enjoy significant electoral success, especially in 2010, but once elected rarely lived up to the rhetoric of their campaigns. They were naturally absorbed into mainstream politics and their ideas just became a part of the establishment.

The Occupy Wall Street movement in 2011 was a left-wing populist movement that rose in the aftermath of the Great Recession, it purportedly was against economic inequality, corporate greed, big finance, and the influence of money in politics. They boasted that their decentralized approach allowed for greater autonomy and avoided their grassroots movement from being co-opted by traditional political interests.

It's most famous and enduring slogan was "we the 99%" - a pithy statement meant to clearly demarcate the haves from the have-nots. The original movement ended inside two months and has been the subject of a great deal of criticism. Among the primary critiques are the conspicuous absence of an agenda that could pragmatically be converted into policy considerations, a fact underscored by the lack of legislative outputs inspired by the movement. In many ways however, that was probably never the point.

'We the 99%' for starters is so broad a category it renders its generalizable characteristics meaningless. No serious-minded person actually believes that the plight and experiences of the bottom quintile of the socioeconomic spectrum are comparable to the top quintile. Placing them in the same group without distinction as the 99% disproportionately focuses on the 1% and spares the great majority of the upper middle class any meaningful level of scrutiny. The demographic composition of the Occupy movement's protests clearly establish the point that their interests had little to do with improving the conditions of the truly marginalized.

The protesters were "relatively affluent: roughly three quarters (72 percent) of participants came from households above the 2011 New York City median. A plurality came from households that brought in over $100k per year. 76 percent of participants had a BA degree or higher". Missing among the protesters were those with blue collar, retail or service jobs, the ones commonly referred to as the working poor. For a movement so ostentatious focused on inequality, the absence of the poor was seemingly overlooked.

The movement did not achieve most of their stated goals but they did significantly disrupt the political and cultural landscape. In many ways they too brought back the politics of anger and outrage establishing the foundation of American left wing identity politics. For the organizers and politicians who supported the movement, many enjoyed some measure of success in endeavours stemming from the movement but rarely lived up to the rhetoric. They were naturally absorbed into mainstream politics and cultural discourse and their ideas just became a part of the establishment.

In both instances the movements extolled ideologies that were out of step with the majority of the electorate, but their outsized influence had a pernicious impact on social discourse. In both instances their messaging was amplified by social media and adopted uncritically as representative by traditional media. America is the third most populous country in the world and the ubiquity of American culture is often ignored given their proficiency and capacity for cultural transmission through popular culture. What might have been fringe ideologies soon came to dominate the social, political, and cultural reproduction of ideas. Obscured in the cultural shift was the slow strangulation of centrist politics.

For the vast majority of people living in liberal democracies, there is acceptance for a balance between state welfare and individual rights. It is premised on the concept of pluralism, toleration, and political participation, supported by the rule of law and an independent judiciary and media. Liberal democracy is a by-product of Enlightenment thinking and was intended as an alternative to autocratic or monarchial governance. Yet increasingly on either end of the political spectrum we appear to have become more prescriptive and ideologically rigid, worse still on both ends the tendency to bemoan heterodoxy in favour of ideological homogeneity appears to have become the default operating system.

The Bio-Psycho-Social

"Human experience suggests, and behavioural economist confirm that the pain of loss exceeds the pleasure of gain. While failing to improve one's well-being is despairing, losing ground is bitter." - William A. Galston

Biologically humans are 99.9% identical at the DNA level, with only 0.1% of variation and most genetic variation is within populations, not between them. Yet we have created arbitrary categories mostly based on phenotypical traits that obscure that reality. While biological race is a fiction, race as a social construct is widely accepted as real. That being said there are very few, if any, ideological characteristics that are uniformly distributed by racial categorization. Much like our genes, there is often more ideological variance within races than between them.

Our psychology leads us to erroneously believe in that which just isn't so. Cognitive biases are a feature not a bug of our cultural dispositions. Negativity bias causes amplified emotional responses to negative events compared to positive events of equal magnitude. Much of today's political discourse occurs online but our predisposition to focus on and scrutinize the negative, more effectively draws our attention and ultimately informs our perceptions. Confirmation bias is particularly present in the consumption of news and media. Personally curated content reinforces echo chambers and makes people cling to sources that support their political orientation.

Socially we appear to have lost our capacity to appreciate nuance. Tribalism is hard wired into the human condition and our evolutionary disposition towards in-group solidarity negatively influences our willingness to compromise, collaborate, and cooperate.

Polarization has steadily worsened over time but in many ways, this is actually an illusory problem created by distortions in our cultural discourse. Both the right and the left wings of our political system have increasingly focused on appealing to a narrow band of the electorate on the edges of the ideological spectrum. It makes for great theatre and certainly helps news ratings but does little to inform the public on actual policy priorities that impact the majority of people, most of whom probably sit closer to the center on political issues. The focus on the edges contributes to deepening social divisions between more and less educated citizens, between those who benefit from technological change and those who are threatened by it.

In short, we didn't just wake up one day and become more earnest in our adherence to rigid ideological fealty. Our bio-psycho-social characteristics provided fertile grounds to plant the seed of division allowing us to sow a bountiful harvest of polarization. On social media 80% of the viral content is created by 10% of users; I fear it is possible that 80% of our political priorities are being co-opted by 10% of the electorate.

Democracy was never intended to be a zero-sum game. The governing party and the opposition both play a vital role. They are meant to advocate and dissent, to debate and compromise, to establish and reform. They are meant to work together for the greater good of all citizens. We the electorate have an important role too, and it is not to pillory each other in the public square. We need to demand more of our politicians, we have to demand more of ourselves. To be informed we need to take the spectacle and theatre out of politics. We need to hold our representatives accountable and demand that they make their case for our vote not merely tell us the other side sucks. Our gradual but consistent shift towards the edges have strangled the centrist and in so doing eroded the essential role of moderation in our politics.

An Ode to Nietzsche
The Centrist is dead. The Centrist remains dead. And we have killed him. How shall we comfort ourselves, now? Moderation, once the holiest and mightiest in the world of political affairs has bled to death under our divisive knives: who will wipe this blood off us? What water is there for us to clean ourselves of this polarization? What festivals of atonement, what sacred games shall we have to invent? Must we ourselves not become The Centrist if for no other reason than to rectify this self-inflicted tragedy?

On Marriage Through a Different Lens

Published by Seeking Veritas on Substack: Jul 30, 2024

"If you spend your life grinding because you think you have to build the perfect future, you will probably achieve almost everything you want, you will surpass the expectations of the past, miss the present and have no one to share the future with." – K.G.

My writing partner and friend Brian Sankarsingh recently published an article about marriage after decades of being together. He discussed the changing tides of time and responsibilities that come as children get older and move on with their lives, as routines and interest change, and as couples get older and find themselves in new stages of life. He has known his wife since they were young and they have spent decades together sharing their lives, raising their children, and supporting each other through this life journey. It is an article that is uplifting and inspiring but also an in-your-face reminder of what could have been for those of us who have tried and failed.

I live on the other end of the marriage spectrum. I have failed not once, not twice, but three times at this sacred tradition. As I round the corner towards the age of 50, I have no concept of what a possible happily ever after might look like. Today I'm a man with a note stuck to his health card that reads, "In the event of an emergency, please rescue my dog who is home alone".

Surpassing The Expectations of the Past

Having grown up in another part of the world, with parents from the immediate post WWII era, I was raised with a seemingly clear sense of purpose, albeit a social concept that would be considered out of date today. From the time I arrived in Canada, I felt like I was a generation behind in mindset and disposition.

Over a lifetime I have internalized and cemented my early socialization; men are providers, stoic and reserved, emotionally constrained with a stiff upper lip, along with all the other stereotypic tropes I'm sure you are all aware about. Yet coming out of high school, I took a job unloading trucks and did not pursue post-secondary education. That worked for me for a couple of years and then the internalized pressure to be more kicked in, my attitude and drive kicked in, I remembered the lessons about work ethic and the virtue of struggle. I had to set aside childish things and become a man. The weekend nightclub scene stopped, the sports car sold, it was time to get serious.

I applied myself, attended post-secondary at night school, began a career and would grind every day with a singular focus on being successful. Over the next thirty years I would complete several post-secondary programs, become a senior manager at a large publicly traded company, parlay that into a career as a post-secondary educator with all the perks of job security, guaranteed pension for life after retirement, and more vacation time than most people can imagine what to do with. But even that wasn't enough, and I was not done, after almost two decades in academia I took on senior management roles, while simultaneously becoming a regular newspaper columnist, an author and a TEDx speaker. I had the house with the pool, the dog, and the overpriced truck I always wanted but didn't actually need.

The overconfident, uneducated, manual labourer who unloaded trucks at eighteen years old should be so proud of what was achieved with focus and grit. I had surpassed the expectations of the past.

Missing the Present

That thirty-year journey was not all sunshine and rainbows, along the way being committed to the hustle and the grind would come with costs. Long work hours, singular focus, and a relentless future orientation didn't always make me the nicest person to be around. For my part, however, I convinced myself that it would all be worth it in the long run. I was sure that my family would benefit from this work ethic and drive, our future selves would see the value of the sacrifices and would reap the dividends of my necessary drive.

Marriage of course was a natural part of the plan. After all, a man provides for his family, he is stoic so as to be calm in crisis, he has a stiff upper lip so adversity can be taken in stride. Being a man, I believed was about service and strength and I liked being the good man in a storm. I was married once in my twenties, once in my thirties, and once in my forties and learned different things from each of those experiences. My first wife was the kindest person, and our marriage was the epitome of companionship built on genuine friendship. We didn't have much but we had everything we needed, and we spent a lot of time doing things that we both enjoyed together. In the fog and folly of youth I believed marriage could be more.

My second wife is the mother of my child, a beautiful boy who I love more than anything in this world. This marriage was the epitome of stability and security. The home in the ideal neighbourhood, the Cadillac, the golden retriever and strolls with the child in his Baby Bjorn. In the fog of ambition, I believed marriage could be more.

My third wife is the most intelligent and independent woman I have ever known, she had long ago mastered the art of making the most out of any situation life threw at her. She encouraged me to pursue my dreams, and I can say unequivocally that without her I would have never done the TEDx Talk or become an author. This marriage also gave me stepchildren who I grew to love like my own. During our marriage we went through a global pandemic, major health issues, blending families, starting businesses and realizing passions. Yet despite all the promise and hope that was on offer, my singular focus on the destination rather than the journey prevented me from appreciating the present. I dedicated so much time, energy and effort to creating the ideal future that I missed the opportunities to appreciate where we were and who we were individually. In the fog of perfection, I believed marriage could be more.

The self-assured, well educated, and well employed man I grew into had missed most of the moments in the present while building the future.

The Future

"A divorce is like an amputation: you survive it, but there's less of you." – Margaret Atwood

Today I live on the other end of the marriage spectrum and I'm often the punch line at the end of every marriage joke. I can probably tell you more than you care to know about how Karl Marx thought marriage in bourgeois society was a farce, or why Durkheim viewed marriage as a protective factor against suicide, I could even wax poetic about how romantic love in the Western tradition originated in the late nineteenth and early twentieth centuries. But I probably cannot tell you very much that is useful about being an actual husband. Too often I offered only logic when empathy was required, only solutions when a sounding board was desired, and only analysis when connection was needed.

As I round the corner toward the back nine of life, I take my coffee every morning on the back deck, overlooking the pool where my stepchildren once swam, my truck on the driveway where two cars once parked, my pension within sight with no one assigned to the survivor benefit. My dog at my feet and my coffee in hand, I can't help but wonder about that fog I routinely got lost within. It seemed like only yesterday the future was a distant destination and then in the blink of an eye life went by.

I kept wanting more and somewhere along the way I lost sight of the fact that the grind was supposed to have been about family, about having a companion to share your dreams and life with when the rat race ended. I overlooked the obvious, that they were supposed to be cherished and appreciated all the way along that journey towards the golden years.

The remorseful man with bookshelves full of wisdom from generations gone by, with framed pictures of accomplishments, has turned into the person who loved and lost, who now sits alone having pushed away anyone that might have been there in the future.

A Better Masculinity
"Don't gain the world and lose your soul; wisdom is better than silver or gold" - Bob Marley

Here's to the beautiful ideal of marriage, with utmost respect to those skilled enough to make it work and wise enough to live in the present and appreciate the presence of those who really matter.

Wisdom came at a higher price than I had ever planned for, because when the music stopped, the temporal constraints of this world had removed the do-over option. A wistful smile often sneaks through when I think about the numerous times I confidently proclaimed, "anyone can do the good days, it's the hard days that matter." Who knew the skill it took to appreciate the good days, not me to be certain. Turns out the purpose of the grind was never to leave behind silver and gold to people who never had a chance to know you.

As I look at my son, I know that I have to redefine masculinity. The world doesn't need just calm men in the storm, it also needs good men who know how to navigate the seas when the waters are calm because that is where the living happens. That is where companionship develops, family is forged, and supportive partners share dreams and aspirations.

Here's to the beautiful ideal of marriage, with utmost respect to those skilled enough to make it work, and wise enough to live in the present and appreciate the presence of those who really matter.

My Profound Fortnight in Moscow

Published by Seeking Veritas on Substack: Jun 27, 2023

I travelled to Russia in 1994 for a cornea transplant; I returned with important life lessons in simplicity, and an appreciation for a common humanity that transcended race, culture, gender, or religion.

A pivotal pitstop on my life journey leading to Canada came in the way of a health crisis. At the age of eleven, I was diagnosed with a hereditary eye disease that could ultimately lead to a complete loss of sight. At the time there did not seem to be any sense of panic; the doctors believed that treatment could wait until my body was done growing. The best estimate back then was that I had until approximately the age of eighteen to twenty-one before this would be a major concern. Life had other plans.

By the time I was a teenager, I had 45% vision in the left eye but only 5% vision in the right. I found myself sitting alone in an ophthalmologist's office discussing what life would be like in a month when I went blind. The doctor explained to me that the cornea in my right eye was so thin that it was at risk of tearing, and when that happened, my retina would get damaged from the exposure.

As I sat there listening to the doctor, I imagined every way in which my life would never be the same again. I remember thinking that at least I was fortunate to have travelled the world; I would need to cement those memories before my world went dark. The thoughts in my head as I left the doctor's office were all-consuming, mostly negative, and positively terrifying.

We sought a second opinion, this time at a private Russian hospital that had opened in Dubai after the fall of the former Soviet Union. The surgeon there confirmed that the first doctor was half correct; I was now two weeks away from being blind. However, he was confident they could perform a successful cornea transplant if only I could get to Moscow immediately. And so, to Russia we went.

My trip was an interesting experience, incomparable to any I had experienced up to that point. My father and I arrived at the airport in Moscow at 3:00 a.m. and the terminal was largely vacant. This was not a bustling airport like so many I had been in before. The walls were a dingy shade of military green, probably painted decades ago and never touched up. The lighting was sparse and dim. The airport was unusually quiet, seemingly abandoned, reminiscent of a place that once was but no longer is. It did not appear like there was a lot of airline traffic through those terminals.

I estimate the customs officer stood about six feet four inches based on how much taller he was compared to me. He had blonde hair visible under his uniform hat, a strong square jaw, ice blue eyes, thin lips, and an expressionless face. He did not smile; I wonder if that had been conditioned out. His tone was neutral, his words plainly matter of fact. He had a job to do, and he was doing it efficiently, if I had something to hide, I think I would have confessed it right there! Either way, our passports were stamped, and we were cleared to go.

A translator arranged by the hospital back in Dubai picked us up at Moscow airport and brought us to the hospital. A sprawling building with all Russian staff but not a single Russian patient visible. My first week there was mostly pre-operation testing, but I managed to squeeze in a little sight-seeing (an ironic term given I was there almost blind). Given the cost of the hospital room per day, we chose to rent a room for the first week. Post operative care would require us to stay in the hospital after my cornea transplant.

A Room That Offered a Different View

The translator arranged for a room we could rent in an apartment near the hospital for the week leading up to the surgery. The family had bought the unit for $100 after the post communist housing blocks were sold off. An enormous amount of money for a family not accustomed to the concept of personal wealth. I had never been in an atmosphere like the one I found myself in.

The building was fourteen stories high with hallways that appeared to be a few miles long. The walls were a dull yellow, the lighting less than optimal. There was no decor to speak of in the lobby, or anywhere else in the building for that matter. The elevator was small, and it creaked and laboured up to the tenth floor where their apartment was located. As I stepped off the elevator, I peered once again at the note from the translator;

Apartment 1017, Pyotr Ivanovich Morozov, followed by a notation $15US/day below it. As I walked down the hallway, I could hear faint chatter coming from the units; privacy was clearly not a concern to whoever built this place.

I passed door after door of perfectly identical woodwork. I arrived at 1017 and knocked twice on the door. I was greeted by a man in his fifties, with weathered lines across his brow, and a warm and inviting smile. He welcomed me in and told me he spoke a sufficient amount of English, but his wife Valentina and daughter Natalya only spoke Russian. They smiled and gestured me into their apartment.

If communism was about pragmatic functionality, their apartment was perfectly analogous. There was no wasted space and every inch of it had a practical purpose. The designer clearly only meant to address the most rudimentary part of Maslow's pyramid. Five of us were now standing inside a very small space; the wife and the daughter stepped back into the kitchen and Pyotr gestured us toward the door on my left. The door was ajar, as I pushed it open, he smiled and nodded. There were two single beds, a small table with a single lamp, and an antique looking alarm clock. It was like something I had only ever seen in the movies.

Across from the bed was a narrow dresser, plain wood, no designs, with three drawers intended for us to use as required.

Once I set my bag down, Pyotr motioned me back towards the front door. He pointed to the door directly beside ours; that was where the three of them would sleep while we were renting his daughter's room. To the right of the front door was another one, visible only when the entrance door was shut. It was the bathroom: a toilet, sink, and small stand-up shower — arguably the smallest bathroom I had ever seen. In front of the main doorway was another room, a cozy kitchen, equipped with old appliances and a small table that seated four people. That was the entirety of the apartment, every inch assigned purpose and function.

My Walk-Through Red Square

Over the fourteen days I spent in Moscow, I took the opportunity to see a sliver of this beautifully complex historical place. Standing in the middle of Red Square appreciating the architecture and culture was fascinating, and especially meaningful given how I believed that my capacity to see the world could forever be altered by the end of the week if anything did not go as planned.

The ornate design utilized in their architecture seemed a perfect veneer obscuring the total tyrannical domination

Dostoyevsky described more than a century earlier. The complexity woven into the fabric of this society was unmistakable.

One cannot help but feel extremely small when standing in the middle of the square. I wondered if that was the intention, and I pondered whether the average Russian citizen felt the same way.

A Walk in the Neighbourhood

I had seen abject poverty many times in my life on my travels, but being up close and personal to it in a new place was humbling all over again. I walked in the neighbourhood to local stores to pick up supplies. The bakery had an extremely long line for day-old bread and almost no one in line for fresh bread, I felt guilt when it occurred to me that no one else in that bakery even glanced over at the line I was in. Vendors sold chicken frozen in large blocks of ice on the street; a machete would hack of a piece of ice containing a frozen chicken if you had the money to purchase one.

The streets had a cold feel to them. People smiled and were courteous to me, but one could sense that life had not delivered on all the promises made when the iron curtain came down only a few years earlier. Turns out the fall of communism was not all sunshine and roses for the average person. Establishing capitalism and democracy was a slow process, not some utopian silver bullet many were made to believe. There was evidence everywhere of wealth inequality. It turns out that society was clearly never equal, and the concept of a unified proletariat was merely an illusory figment of the propaganda machine.

A Language Without Words

Natalya was about the same age as me. That entire week we hung out every evening, playing cards, going for walks with her dog, meeting up with her friends, and sitting around the kitchen table passing the time. The incredible thing was that we could not speak the same language, given she did not understand English, and I could not communicate in Russian; and we probably had no common life experiences or culture. Yet we found a way to cooperate and coexist in a small space. Just two young people who managed to play card games, laugh, and smile without words, connected only by our common humanity and the innocent disposition seemingly unique to youthful innocence.

Looking back, I appreciate the simplicity of those interactions. We did not think about race, gender, religion, or culture; we were just two people, happy to have some company and mutually willing to find a way to communicate as humans in a shared world. The next year, I would immigrate to Canada. As I would discover, those moments in Russia would be some of the simplest interactions I would have when confronted with new culture, traditions, and people.

My Glass House of Faith & Folly

Published by Seeking Veritas on Substack: Jul 20, 2024

"I don't really believe in God, but I'd like to think there is something after this [life], it can't just be nothingness."

It was 2011 and my son's arrival into this world was only a few months away. I would be a father soon and the weight of this life altering decision would challenge the very foundations of my world view; it would make me question the nonchalance with which I had infrequently questioned my own socio-religious disposition. All that inner turmoil was kicked off with a five-word question exchanged with his mother: "Should we baptize the child?"

Ancestrally my family is from India. My roots within that society more specifically can be traced back to one of the smallest states in the country, an area bordered by the Arabian Sea on its western coast, a region of India colonized by the Portuguese between the years 1510 to 1961 (for those who don't know, that's 14 years past Indian independence from British rule). As a direct result of Portuguese subjugation my family, along with most others from that region, carry the legacy of colonization through our Portuguese last names and of course, our adherence to Catholicism.

I was raised Roman Catholic by devoutly Christian parents, surrounded by family who unquestioningly accepted their faith alongside the prerequisite doctrine, dogma, and rituals prescribed by the church. I attended Catechism, served mass as an altar-boy, received all my sacraments, studied at a Catholic school, and attended weekly mass with my family and friends. Like most people who are assigned their religion at birth, it was a reality I didn't question. I accepted without introspective examination that I was obviously born by cosmic lottery into the only true religion. Of course, it never occurred to me as a child that every single religious person regardless of their theistic background made the exact same leap of faith, every one of them also born by cosmic lottery into the one true religion, only it was the religion of their family history.

Questioning faith, religion, or even practice was unheard of in my family. I suppose there was strict adherence to the idea that blessed are those who have not seen and yet believe. Yet by the time I was ready to raise a child in this world, the tacit acceptance of religious ideology absent critical reflection seemed misguided to me.

My son's mother was Christian, however, through early courtship and subsequent marriage, the conversation about religion had never come up. In all fairness, neither one of us had attended church service in years. After high school I had slowly transitioned over time from a practicing Catholic, to a ceremonial Catholic (you know, the ones who attend church service twice a year, for Christmas and Easter), and then to a Catholic by association only, who stepped into a church solely for weddings and funerals. Now with a child on the way, we sat down to have the discussion about whether we would baptize our child and what, if any, religious tradition we would raise him within.

Rabbit Holes

I had shared my lack of participation in religious service with my son's mother, as well as my quiet discomfort with dogma in general. She on the other hand, expressed a sentiment I wouldn't come to appreciate for many years. She expressed that she didn't practice and wasn't sure that she believed in God, but couldn't reconcile that with a sense of nothingness that might follow death. Nonetheless, she left the decision with me and in keeping with one of my consistent follies, I went down a rabbit hole looking for answers to questions I had previously never examined. I was fuelled by an insatiable curiosity, supported by a library of books, and a commitment to keep an open mind.

My rabbit hole turned into a journey of discovery that would last several years, span hundreds of books, debates, podcasts, videos, and articles, traversing everything from Animism to Scientology, from Greek philosophy to Stoicism, from Zoroastrianism to Mormonism. I even spent a little time trying to understand upper middle class white women committed to Ashtanga Yoga, Chai Tea, and understanding their vibrations so they could align their Chakras. I didn't have the heart back then to tell them that Chai was the Indian word for tea, and so their beverage order was quixotically redundant. I will admit that I was never able to wrap my mind around that last group. To the best of my understanding, Lululemon supplies the uniforms, Yeti sponsors the hydration, and TikTok fuels the inspiration. But I confess I was unable to learn anything more.

Things You Didn't Know You Didn't Know

Turns out Catechism barely covered the history of Catholicism. They seemed to have cherry-picked select stories and created a seemingly coherent narrative around them, while leaving out a great deal of inconvenient history, including the political involvement of the church, or the very worldly development of canonical law. I was equally baffled by the similarities of mythological stories across time and space. Little seemed original or unique. From virgin births and stars in the east, disciples and betrayal, to crucifixion and resurrection, the themes kept repeating themselves.

Horus (3000 BCE / Egyptian Mythology) – Born of a virgin accompanied by a star in the east, began his ministry at the age of thirty, had twelve disciples, performed miracles and healed the sick. He was betrayed, crucified and resurrected three days later.

Mithra (1200 BCE / Persian Mythology) – Born of a virgin, had twelve disciples, performed miracles. He died, was buried, and resurrected three days later.

Krishna (900 BCE / Indian Mythology) – Born of a virgin accompanied by a star in the east, performed miracles with his disciples. Died and was resurrected.

Dionysus (500 BCE / Greek Mythology) – Born of a virgin, travelling teacher who performed miracles, died and was resurrected.

Jesus (33 CE) – Born of a virgin, accompanied by a star in the east, began his ministry at age thirty, had twelve disciples, travelling teacher who performed miracles and healed the sick. He was betrayed by

Judas, was crucified, placed in a tomb, and resurrected three days later.

Even the staple flood narratives were eerily similar across traditions. While the Genesis account of Noah's Ark is probably the most commonly known today, the flood motif can be found almost identically in other faiths. The obvious example is the Sumerian Epic of Gilgamesh dating back nearly 5,000 years, but similar stories of watery mass destruction and salvation exist in Indian Vedic lore, in Aztec culture, and in creation myths from Egypt to Scandinavia, some involving floods that purge and then remake the earth and humanity.

I was lost. Everything I thought I knew seemed incomplete. I felt duped and disillusioned; how could the people I trusted have kept me in the dark about so much? I was never clear on how to navigate which verses were literal and which were allegorical — as a child, no one would tell me. I had no idea what Pauline Christianity was, nor its divergence from the Jewish reformation that Jesus actually sought. If you told me that the most influential person in the creation of Christianity as we know it today was a man who never met Jesus, whose teachings were at odds with Peter and James, and whose entire doctrine was predicated on a vision, I would have been completely dumbfounded.

As a student in a Catholic school, asking questions about inconsistencies was seen as blasphemy itself. Is this what religion demands? Blind conformity to the beliefs of my ancestors? Is this how I am supposed to raise my soon to be born child?

I never did baptize my child, convinced it was the first step in ensuring I did not indoctrinate him. I was pleased with my decision and never regretted it. Then one day twelve years later, I was driving with him in the passenger seat. I shared with him the premise of Pascal's Wager; he turned to me and said, "I know how I would bet, that's simple, we don't believe in God." It was in that moment that I realized I had indoctrinated him, only I traded Catholicism with Atheism. He had uncritically accepted the things he heard me say, and he did not question the validity of my positions. I unwittingly did the very thing I sought to avoid.

The Mast & Not the Anchor

"For the non-believer, no evidence is ever enough and for the believer, no evidence is ever required."

Today I accept that there is something ineffable about faith and the old maxim is instructive here, "For the non-believer, no evidence is ever enough and for the believer, no evidence is ever required." Religion as a social institution provides a language, identity, and community. Through shared symbols and metaphors, it provides a common language for believers and in so doing, creates a sense of belonging and purpose for a great number of individuals.

All around us are people who speak different languages, share different mythologies designed to help their young learn ancient wisdom, practice different rituals, use different symbols, and work diligently towards living their best lives in search of a higher purpose. Some call that purpose God; others Allah, Yahweh, Brahma, Shiva or Vishnu. Others still think of it as Nirvana, or the purpose of a life well lived. We sometimes fail to recognize that the people we can't seem to understand are actually working towards the same purpose, with similar conviction; only they are speaking in another language, using different symbols, rituals, and metaphors to communicate amongst each other about that which is ineffable to us all.

Anthropologists have uncovered artifacts from pre-historic societies that indicate a practice of ritual and worship. Burial sites, art, and places of worship practices that pre-date modern societies and any known world religion. Author and scholar Reza Aslan often states that there appears to be a tendency hard wired into humans to humanize and anthropomorphize the divine. Perhaps there is validity in the philosophizing of David Hume and Ludwig Feuerbach who thought that religions, especially primitive religions, sprang from the natural curiosity about the future constantly encumbered with hopes and fears. Perhaps religion provided the language to give hope in the face of our natural limitations. A hope that nothingness was not the end of the journey. I began to understand what my son's mother was alluding to, hope that purpose was greater than our capacity to understand.

Religion is infinitely malleable and adaptable to social circumstances and as such, has constantly evolved to meet the norms and needs of societies in every epoch. Religion in many ways is a human endeavour to bring meaning to the uncertainty of the unknown. The French sociologist Emile Durkheim rejected the supernatural basis of religion but argued that it provided a collective consciousness, a social adhesive that fosters cohesion, and enables and maintains social solidarity. It may be the reason so many people accept that not knowing is sufficient and faith is inspiring.

Nothing in my childhood drew my attention to the rich diversity of religious views and practices. All of them believing that their scriptures, traditions, and history are the proper interpretation of a true deity. I came to appreciate over time the richness and beauty of the storytelling at the heart of every major religious tradition. After all, storytelling is the essence of being human, it is how our shared experiences and wisdom has been passed down for millennia.

Facts get forgotten, reinterpreted, and altered over time, but stories are how we keep this human journey alive. Along my journey of self-discovery, I didn't find THE answer, but I recognized that my role as a father was to be my son's mast and not his anchor. Replacing one ideology with another is merely indoctrination by another name. I needed to do better, I needed to guide my son on how to think, not what to think. It's a work in progress and it's also a lifelong journey that will make for a great story that he might one day share with his progeny.

I'm still not a believer, but I have a greater respect for those who are.

Swiping, Sorting, Browsing — But Not Dating

Published by Seeking Veritas on Substack: Jun 5, 2024

I don't take long walks on the beach, as there are no long beaches by the lake where I live. Also can't argue that hiking Machu Picchu wouldn't make for a great date although I tend to start with coffee, might have something to do with the kid, and the dog, and the job, and the house, also the alimony, and the child support, but maybe skydiving and Rocky Mountain climbing might be a closer option than Peru... if only I could live like I was dying. Pesky retirement planning keeps getting in the way!

I don't really need to know your dietary restrictions; I affirm your right to order whatever floats your boat off the menu. On a related note, thanks for sharing your gym schedule, it may be less indicative about who you are than say your voting preferences, but definitely a nice to know.

I would never tell you I'm looking for a long-term relationship because I lost my crystal ball in 1986 and have long ago accepted that I have no idea where anything is going, also I haven't yet met you! But really, imagine how creepy it would be if someone actually read you the standard profile information on a first date! Jeez, you'd probably tell them to slow their roll at least until the scone arrived.

What can I say, I am a Middle-aged Gen Xer; skeptical about technology when not filtered through an economic lens, with a low tolerance for virtue signalling; Want to meet for a coffee and unpack that?

Alright, that might make you laugh if I said it in person, but probably not the best profile bio on a dating app! Pretty sure that would get a "swipe left" reaction by most dating app users. Perhaps therein lies the problem, dating apps lack context.

A Pew Research study found that 45% of people who used dating apps recently said they "left them feeling more frustrated than hopeful." The irony of that statement is unavoidable given apps like Tinder have approximately 75 million active users, despite only being in business for around 12 years, and Tinder is only one of many dating apps out there on the market. The proliferation of dating apps tracks consistently with the ubiquity of computer mediated modes of communication that we have wholeheartedly embraced in the 21st century, but at what cost have we prioritized convenience over connection?

Annie Lord, a freelance writer based out of London writing for the Guardian, discussed the challenges inherent with dating apps in her 2022 article "'Why am I talking to 10 guys?' The rise and fall of dating apps." She highlights that the rate at which people download and delete dating apps is second only to online gambling. That is a business model that works extremely well for the tech companies designing these apps. It is a strategy that is strikingly similar to the approach taken by the multi-billion-dollar diet industry, keep the customer coming back but never actually deliver on the promise to improve their lives. Both industries sell an illusion propped up on emotional manipulation and utilize outliers to demonstrate their capacity to transform people's actual experience.

In her article, Lord points out that it has "become so normalised to look for dates through apps now that we've forgotten how to approach people in person. We worry if it's inappropriate, if we might say something wrong or that the other person isn't interested. On an app you can see on the profile what a person is looking for, something serious or casual. It's all about communication and without apps maybe we'd have to relearn these social cues." She wonders if we could actually go back to life before dating apps, before starting conversations with strangers in public was considered cringy.

Of course, the odds are stacked greatly against those in both camps, dating app users and those hoping for an old school approach.

For those on the dating apps, a little-known fact to many users is that there is a disproportionately larger number of men on most sites. A recent study suggested that the average man has to send approximately 144 messages in order to get a single reply. Conversely, women rated as attractive are bombarded with constant messages requiring them to become increasingly exclusionary with their interactions. At the crossroads of those two experiences is the making of a highly transactional arrangement. The more messages a man has to send the more McDonaldized they become, and the more cookie cutter they appear, the less likely women are to select them. What a terrible confluence of circumstances.

For those hoping for the old school fairytale — catching an eye across the room, a smile and an awkward approach, a fumbly mess of a conversation until a laugh breaks through, and then that glimmer of hope that you may get asked out — that scene is more reminiscent of a movie these days. Many men I've spoken to are nervous about making the first move. The media portrayal of the #MeToo movement is still relatively fresh and even the most upstanding among us worry about being falsely accused of impropriety. For both men and women self consciousness about appearance has always existed, self doubt and self-esteem issues have always made dating difficult, but a smile had a way of cutting through those limiting beliefs. Hard to get a smile when we have changed the social scripts so much, people feel constantly monitored and chastised for every social faux pas. Worse still, there are no smiles to be had on an app, at least until someone swipes right. And just so we are clear, nothing in this paragraph is meant to excuse actual bad behaviour, bad actors, abusive and coercive acts, sexism or misogyny.

Leah Asmelash, a culture writer for CNN, quotes Benson Zhou, an assistant professor at New York University Shanghai who studies sexuality and digital media in her 2023 article "How dating apps 'ruined dating' for some." Zhou posits that while dating has always been superficial, the difference now is a fixation on physical appearance, profile data points, and rapid sorting: "[T]he first thing you see while swiping is a picture... Even if you match with a variety of people — sparking optimism — the probability of actually connecting with that person is relatively low, ... leading to feelings of exhaustion or alienation."

Moreover, dating apps serve to dehumanize and decontextualize actual people by transforming them into commodities and data points lost in a sea of supposed options who are only a swipe away. When innumerable options are apparently available it makes the individual on the screen less valuable, more expendable, and completely transactional. No wonder ghosting is so common and dismissiveness the default. Can you imagine an in-person environment where someone initiated a conversation and you responded with, "I don't like your face"!

With everything we know, why are dating apps still so popular? Are people still hopelessly romantic in search of their soulmates, or is the dopamine rush from a match hopelessly addictive?

Layer over the challenges outlined above with identity-based intersections like age, ethnicity, culture, religion, and racial categorizations and you complicate the situation further. In an age of connectivity and access, we seem to have little of either with the people around us.

We Are All Just People on a Mountain

Published by Seeking Veritas on Substack: Dec 30, 2023

Have you ever known a person who spends a lot of time living in their head? A person lost somewhere between being a dreamer and being a loner. People like that exist and other people either want to save them or outright avoid them. I am one of those people and I've been that way for as long as I can remember.

There is a perpetual push and pull, fuelled by curiosity, always raging in my mind. It makes me a tired, restless soul but it also satiates the creative misfit within, and that's a beast I'm not ready to abandon yet. To me, the world is a complex puzzle, an enigma wrapped in a riddle surrounded by a mystery. There are clues everywhere I look waiting to be discovered, patterns and contradictions to be decoded, multiple perspectives to consider, knowledge to be imbibed, and wisdom to acquire.

I have been criticized for failing to appreciate the simple things and I'm routinely reminded of my frequently expressed disdain for the mundane. These are charges I cannot easily dismiss, there is reliable record of my rants on the subject! I am, after all, that person who responds "thank-you," when referred to as a disrupter or a constructive deviant. Some have cautioned that those are not compliments but the badges offered to the expendables, the useful idiots who challenge the status quo in the service of a greater good, only to be forgotten as a foot note lost in history. The credit for fixing the broken status quo laid bare by the expendable usually goes to the charismatic orator in the fine suit. That does not bother me much.

I'm more interested in the lessons from history than the unending cast of characters who occupy the limelight for a fraction of a second in the grand scale of time. It is only the lessons that may prevent us from repeating the errors of the past. The folly of hubris is fairly consistent and well documented across time and space; it provides satisfactory explanations for most human foibles and failures. If only we were more committed to open dialogue and vicarious learning available from the past, we may more readily discover our capacity for empathy, mutual respect, and perhaps even that elusive truth always lingering on the horizon.

The Tyranny of the Minority

A significant amount of ink has been spilled on the subject of polarization in 2024, although it's hardly a new topic. A lot has been said about the people on the far left being hyper-woke and people on the far right being ethnocentric. We did a retro-rewind and saw arguments in favour of segregation — sorry, affinity groups having safe spaces to only socialize with similarly pigmented individuals. Earlier in the year, the anti-woke squad put some points up on the board when black Jesus (no, not Michael Jordan) had his anti-racist centre in Boston get bad press for its poor management and underperformance. But the woke finished strong in Canada with a proposal to amend federal law to consider black people distinct and separate from other people of colour. Separate but equal, I'm sure!

We saw some gay men being pushed out of the LGBTQ ally group because their positionality overlapped with being white and male; never mind that they were previously criminalized merely for who they loved or were attracted to (they sometimes liked sex without love! GASP! What heathens, heterosexuals would never do that... Wait!).

Society took on the feminists who demonstrated their bigotry when asserting that a woman couldn't have a penis. We also added to the inclusive lexicon with terms like birthing people, chest feeders, and menstrual equity. Not to be outdone, the race essentialists coined the term white-adjacent to clearly distinguish between the equity-deserving and the undeserving, I presume.

We saw protests about schools notifying parents about issues related to their children who are minors, the argument being parents are potentially dangerous and often don't provide safe spaces for their own children who may be questioning their sexuality. The solution: confiding in school teachers about important stages of psycho-sexual development. What could go wrong with keeping secrets from family and trusting government run schools to decide the best interest of children?

I even heard an unverified rumour that we may amend the age Canadian children can legally emancipate themselves from their parents from 16 to 12. The parents/guardians will still be financial responsible for the emancipated minor, but the local school boards will provide a safe space to validate their experience. (I'm not confirming the validity of that rumour, but you should thank post-modernism if you are unclear on the objective reality here.)

We saw impassioned protests about 70+ year old regional conflicts on the other side of the world, from a lot of people who know nothing about Golda Meir, Yitzhak Rabin, Yasser Arafat, or any lessons that could be gleaned from that accord struck in Oslo, overseen by Slick Willy, you know, before we became more interested in the blowjobs he received under that fine desk made from the timbers of the British ship, the H.M.S. Resolute. That gift from Queen Victoria to President Rutherford B. Hayes in 1880 has seen a lot! Although in all fairness, I'm not sure how many of those protestors would know what shaped room houses that desk. Ironically, they could probably name the person who gave that blowjob, if only they could understand the contents of this paragraph.

I will leave the recap at the tip of the iceberg; suffice it to say the rest of the year offered a lot more that could have made the highlight reel. Now, if only we took a moment to recognize that social media and that which is trending over-represents the margins, we would realize that most of us are situated somewhere in the middle of that ideological spectrum. So, while the VERY vocal minority dominates the poles, there is a lot of space for us to find common humanity, shared purpose, mutual respect, and community among the silent majority.

Seeking Veritas

We are all so caught up in our own lives, our own ideals, and our own tribes, that we don't recognize when we ourselves become dogmatic, pious, and ideologically rigid. We are all guilty of it at times, because we are all human. Therein lies the answer to our problem, — we are all human, including those we disagree with.

I once visited a Sikh gurdwara and spoke with a gyani about belief. He shared a metaphor with me that has stuck with me for decades and helped me find common ground in the most unlikely spaces. Allow me to share it with you.

He described life, and by extension our world, like a mountain. On every side of the mountain there are people who speak different languages; they share different mythologies that are designed to help their young learn ancient wisdom, they practice different rituals, use different symbols, and work diligently towards living their best lives. The peak of the mountain represents the final destination, atop awaits a higher purpose. Some call it God, others Allah, Yahweh, Elohim, Brahma, Shiva or Vishnu. Others still think of it as Nirvana, or the purpose of a life well lived.

Along the way to that final destination, many seems to be trying to live their best lives and be the best person they can be. All of them making mistakes, falling short, and trying again and again. The only problem is that the mountain is so big, we often don't see the people on the other side. We sometimes fail to recognize that the people we can't seem to understand on the other side are actually working towards the same purpose, with similar conviction; only they are speaking in another language, using different symbols, rituals, and metaphors to communicate amongst each other about that which is ineffable to us all.

Maybe we would all benefit from seeing others as just humans on the same cosmic journey. It may require us to be open to listening, open to learning, open to understanding, and maybe even open to disagreeing. Or perhaps we just simply need to be open to those on "the other side" of the mountain. Perhaps we should remember that bad habit we all have, the tendency to judge others by their actions but ourselves by our intentions.

Sometimes my search for the contemporary Rosetta Stone has contributed to my restlessness, more often it has fuelled my curiosity and energized my creativity. I hope 2024 brings us closer to appreciating our common humanity. I hope it allows us to share ideas and respect each other even when we disagree, so that we may better understand each other, better listen to each other, and better communicate with each other.

Here's to finding more common ground in 2024. Whether you are a restless soul, a creative misfit, or somewhere in between, I wish you a Happy New Year!

On Representation and Belonging

Published by Seeking Veritas on Substack: Dec 20, 2023

I had an engaging conversation on the subject of representation today. Someone said it was "critically important" for the organization I work for to hire more people who look like me so that I could see myself represented in my work community. She argued that it could help me feel a sense of belonging.

I'm sure she meant well. In fact, I wholeheartedly believe she was being sincere and well intentioned. A more cynical person may have taken her comment to be performative, but I honestly believe she was trying to be supportive of me in that moment. Nonetheless, several thoughts went racing through my mind. When she said more people who look like me, I wondered what exactly she meant. I was equally perplexed by the idea that this person assumed I must not feel like I belonged at my workplace.

There is a lot to unpack in those thoughts. First, "like me" is an ambiguous abstraction. Like me physically, psychologically, ideologically, politically, emotionally, or intellectually? A degree of specificity would be required so as to evaluate the success of this undertaking. I would argue that I'm more likely to find common ground with someone with similar intellectual curiosity, I may be more comfortable with someone who shares my political ideology, or someone who is psychologically compatible with me, but I'm uncertain how they could screen for that. I know this, however: merely matching someone to my exterior features would be the least meaningful way to find a representative workmate.

Second, why would I not feel like I belonged? That would have been an odd comment if it wasn't so overused in the contemporary workplace. If I needed everyone to look like me in my workplace, an easier strategy might have been to not move to Canada in the first place. Let's face it, there are a lot more Indians in

India; one would imagine I would feel a greater sense of belonging there, until you realize that I've never lived in India, although my parents did. I cannot speak any of the over 100 languages or dialects spoken in India, the only language I speak is English. Nor do I subscribe to any of the major faiths practiced in India. If you factor all that in, you may be able to comprehend why I still have a greater sense of belonging at my workplace than I would if I was transferred to a hypothetical Indian branch office.

In an August 2023 article for Pop Matters, Amir Zaki took on this very subject. He raised important questions about what representation really means, especially when people use the phrase "representation matters" as a conversation ender rather than a means of inviting dialogue. Zaki describes the unreflective manner in which people absorb and then regurgitate ideological arguments without critically evaluating the proposition, inevitably resulting in reductive pithy statements that fail to have any meaningful impact. In his article Zaki states:

"This is at the heart of why I argue that 'Representation Matters' is a shallow slogan that's been weaponized and, at best, is but a partial truth. It's not only an incomplete concept, but if believed and endorsed as intended, it has the potential to harm more than help marginalized people.

"What really 'matters' is that impressionable people are exposed to various perspectives, belief systems, cultures, languages, moral frameworks, ideas, beauty, art, lifestyles, and socio-economic statuses. If, when someone stated that 'representation matters,' but they meant 'ideological diversity matters' — really anything more than superficial diversity — I would be fully on board. But that is simply not the case... we ought to intentionally seek out ideas and behaviors that differ from ours culturally, ethnically, and socio-economically to learn and understand more about the world. We ought to be 'culturally appropriating' with fervor and passion! How absurd it would be if I were to limit my exposure or potential to the ideas and customs of people who share my phenotype and/or ancestry."

My conversation with the well-meaning woman ended well. Our conversation remained respectful and constructive. I appreciated that she felt comfortable engaging with me on the subject, and I appreciated that she made me feel comfortable to express my thoughts. We realized we both belonged right where we were, and our mutual commitment to our work and our community helped us see representation and reflection in each other. Turns out our sense of belonging came from the common humanity and purpose we shared, rather than superficial characteristics that differentiated us.

Why the Obsession with Living in the Present?

Published by Seeking Veritas on Substack: Jul 5, 2023

"I am not someone who was born with knowledge. I simply love antiquity, and diligently look there for knowledge." – Confucius, 551-479 BCE

"This is the dumbest generation that has ever walked the planet," said every preceding generation throughout time. The simplicity of our world view is captured aptly in the circular discussions about generational differences.

Every single generation thinks the one before them were lacking and the one after them lost. Gen Zs will get there too. There is a certain predictability to human behaviour that time has proven repeatedly.

"The past is gone, and the future doesn't exist yet, so be present and live in the moment…"

Some version of the quote above is commonly in circulation at any given time. "Live in the moment" has to be one of the most overused phrases, typically infused with pseudo-profundity masquerading as gravitas by motivational speakers and self-indulgent amateur writers. (Honestly, you should unsubscribe to my digital publication the day I tell you that today is yesterday's tomorrow. At that point, I may just be at the bottom of the creative barrel.) But the truth is always more complicated.

The present is a by-product of the past, and a variable influencing the future. There is a continuity across time that we often take for granted at best or ignore at worst.

Given history has demonstrated that we humans are predictable and seemingly inextricably predisposed to bad decision-making, you would think we would be more willing to learn from the past, rather than live obliviously in the present. We would benefit from seeing the various generations as teammates in a cosmic relay race.

Our predecessors handed us the baton, filled with knowledge, experience, and lessons learned. It is incumbent on us to take the next generation as far as we can before handing off the baton, replete with revised lessons learned, new mistakes, new opportunities and a greater understanding of our complex world. No one in their right mind should want to throw away that knowledge baton and start over. We really don't have to personally make every mistake over again to learn its consequence. Why are we so accepting of vicarious trauma but so opposed to vicarious learning?

Kong Fuzi, known to Westerners as Confucius, lived in ancient China from 551 BCE until 471 BCE. He placed a high value on the relational nature of human beings and believed that virtuous living starts in the family. He taught that being an excellent human was synonymous with being an excellent community member. He philosophically viewed the community and society as larger extensions of family. For this reason, he put a great deal of emphasis on early socialization within the family and considered it central to human development. Based on his view of social relationships he argued that one's public, social, and political life were mere extensions of their natural family life. Many years after this death, China adopted his teachings as their official state philosophy; culture and society based on tradition and family values.

Somehow in contemporary speak we have turned the phrase "family values" into a conservative dog whistle and therefore shun anything that is apparently carried around in some sort of knapsack that is not visible. I'm yet to actually meet anybody who doesn't espouse the virtue of a positive family; fewer still who see no value in community. And almost no one who could even imagine turning back the clock on all the progress made by those who came before us.

Were they wrong about some things? Of course they were! Do you think the next generation will think this current one did everything right?! Let's call that last one rhetorical.

So, maybe we shouldn't always live in the moment. Perhaps we should stop and recognize the men and women upon whose shoulders the present has been built; then reflect on why we are trying to make society better given our relatively short stay on this planet.

The Departed: A Tribute to a Fellow Traveller

Published by Seeking Veritas on Substack: Oct 10, 2023

One day you're sitting on a roof top patio having lunch, talking about writing books, starting a book club, discussing collaborative projects, and figuring out the best days to do your monthly lunch get togethers. A couple of weeks later you're reading a message telling you your friend is gone.

The search for meaning is generally futile; some questions just remain unanswered. An anticlimactic conclusion to a friendship cut short by an unpredictable life event. Reprieve is only found in the memories remaining. The conversations once had, the plans once made that will never come to fruition. A friend gone, a confidant lost; that's one less friendly face I will pass, in the days that will inevitably come, and necessarily pass.

Mourning is an interesting experience. There is sadness and loss, regret over things left unsaid and conversation left with a pin in them, ones you can no longer go back to that will forever remain unfinished. Then insidiously, imposter syndrome wraps jaundiced tentacles: how can I grieve when there are so many who were closer, who probably hurt deeper. There are so many who were around longer, whose memories span decades.

But grief is unpredictable, and it does not neatly organize itself in order of importance. It just needs to be experienced in whatever way feels right.

For us outliers and misfits, camaraderie is rare; genuine connections are few and far between. There was comfort sitting around the small table, in those high back chairs arranged in a circle, sipping coffee, having a natter, and finding comfort in friendship, laughter, and conversation on challenging days. A fellow traveller on life's journey, bonded together with a shared identity we called constructive deviance, characterized by a willingness to cause discomfort with the primary objective of challenging and improving the status quo.

The generosity of spirit, the kindness of word, the lack of pretension characterized his being and is the memory that remains. He will always be larger than life, a true free spirit, who shared his Indigenous heritage with pride and always made room for others to join his circle. He was the best kind.

In the end there is no right way to grieve. Life is unpredictable and there is never a guarantee of tomorrow. Now all that is left is to raise a glass and offer a toast: here's to those, whose presence enrich others, whose passing leaves a void, and whose memory still produces a smile.

Long may your big jib draw! Ride on, b'y! Here's to the Departed!

Snake Oil Salesman or Pastel Artist

Published by Seeking Veritas on Substack: Jan 11, 2024

"Capitalism is the worst economic system, except for all the others."– Says everyone while misquoting Winston Churchill quoting someone else about democracy in some House of Commons speech.

"I am an unapologetic capitalist." How often do you hear a phrase like that from people under the age of 40 in North America? I have an opinion about that; I know, shocking!

For starters, age 40 captures the oldest in the millennial generation and all the Gen Zs now in high school. More relevantly, it captures those in the age of the smart phone and social media influencers. Too young to care about Marshall McLuhan, yet technologically addicted enough to demonstrate that the medium is the message.

I smile at the irony and tragic comedy on full display when someone wearing retro AIR Jordans, carrying a Lululemon cross body bag, and sipping out of a Stanley Quencher H2.0 FlowState containing 40oz of a quad long shot salted caramel mocha latte with two pumps of white chocolate mocha, half whole milk and half breve with no whipped cream, extra foam, extra caramel drizzle, extra salt, and a scoop of vanilla bean powder with light ice well stirred, lectures strangers about the perils of consumerism and the evils of capitalism. I admit it's more obnoxious when you are directly behind them in line at Starbucks, but still somehow equally entertaining.

Remember all those commercials about the evils of bottled water and the plastic pollution? I guess the Stanley Quencher H2.0 FlowState means no more plastic (as long as you can afford the cup… in all the pretty pastel colours… because how can anyone keep reusing just one reusable mug?) I haven't got the memo yet, but I think YETI is out and Stanley is in now.

Regardless of how you feel about the cup itself, you have to appreciate the business savvy behind the marketing and the company's ability to stay relevant after more than 100 years in business. Over a period of three years, the company went from $73 million to over $750 million in sales — now that's revenue growth.

What is more impressive is that they did it by reviving a discontinued line that failed once before, without creating anything new or innovative to the product itself. Unless you consider adding pastel colours revolutionary. For Stanley, it was!

The company changed their target demographic from working blue collar men with a need for a durable thermos, to suburban female millennials and Gen Zs who need to signal their conformity to the latest viral trends.

Now, I've heard people talk about influencers like clairvoyant forecasters who will help you identify the current (albeit fleeting) symbols of your pop cultural relevance. But in all reality, it's a socially engineered cultural relevance sponsored by corporations and sold by "truth tellers" who influence you with their honest and unbiased affiliation with the overpriced brands you just must have too. I don't have a problem with any of that; corporations exist to make a profit. It's the gullible public with their willful blindness that annoys me.

Would a teenage girl or young women buy a Stanley if they saw the old construction commercial? Would they care about the utility of having the lid double as a cup? Well of course not, so a new strategy was employed. Ever notice that social media influencers share their content for free? Andrew Lewis the Freelance Content Marketing Strategist would tell you,

"If you are not paying for it, you're not the customer; you're the product being sold." Social media influencers sell you, the consumer, to the companies by manufacturing demand.

Stanley also partnered with companies like Olay and Starbucks to tap into the customers who already use or align with the symbols of virtue signalling on offer. Stanley's VP of brand marketing Jenn Reeves said in an interview:

"The Stanley Quencher has transcended a water bottle and become a lifestyle accessory… we combine [functionality] with color that they can match with their clothes, their nails…"

According to media sources, Stanley leaned heavily and unabashedly into gender-based marketing when many companies sought to be gender neutral in their strategy to avoid public shaming. Stanley seems to have embraced the social media influencer as a means of engaging would-be customers. They collaborated with influencers and other popular brands, which brought them approximately 10 million views. They drove new interest constantly by encouraging consumers to buy the latest colour. As an added bonus, people have a tendency to take pictures of everything they buy, which then serves as free advertising for the company.

Stanley owes the success of the Quencher H2.0 FlowState in large part to Ashlee LeSueur, Taylor Cannon, and Linley Hutchinson, who own and run The Buy Guide, an e-commerce blog and Instagram account, where the Quencher tumbler was among the first products they featured:

"We promise you, it will sell. We will introduce this cup to an army of other influencers on Instagram, and it will blow your mind what women selling to women looks like... Every time we linked it, it would sell out so quickly... We got so many pictures from teachers who all have them in their classrooms and from nurses stations with cups overflowing in different colors, and we knew we were onto something." – **Ms. Ashlee LeSueur**

The bloggers were able to convince women and girls everywhere that they needed to fit in, they needed to hydrate, and they needed to do it from a pretty pastel cup! How convincing were they? Stanley would know they were so convincing because it brought them $677 million dollars. The best part was they got all that extra money by convincing a bunch of people they have to line up and buy the same product the company has made for decades.

A Forbes article presented data from recent studies showing that influencer marketing is worth approximately $15 billion annually. Yet there is almost no oversight or regulation compared to traditional advertising. Psychological manipulation, high speed internet, and uninformed consumers contribute to the perfect conditions for rapid revenue growth or at least another opportunity to dupe a gullible market.

My suggestion: get informed and then buy whatever you want no matter how frivolous because you choose it. Or at least don't conform to every passing trend, because you know us unapologetic capitalists are coming for you.

Limiting Beliefs: Fact or Fiction

Published by Seeking Veritas on Substack: Dec 12, 2023

I have always loved the story about Roger Bannister and the four-minute mile; I have retold it in classes I have taught too many times too count. I'm drawn to the story because it's about someone who dared to do what others thought impossible. If you read past the immediate story of his accomplishment, however, you discover an even more instructive narrative that highlights the influence of limiting beliefs and the potential to be realized once they are set aside.

For almost 70 years runners and coaches had been seriously and systematically trying to break the four-minute mile. From roughly 1886, the most talented athletes in North America, Europe, and Australia strategized about what it would take to pull off the feat. The experts agreed the conditions would need to be near perfect, and they theorized about the precise conditions under which the record could be broken. Perfect weather, 68 degrees with no wind, on a hard dry clay track, in front of a huge, boisterous crowd urging the runner to his best-ever performance.

On May 6, 1954, on a cold day, on a wet track, in front of a small crowd in Oxford, England, Roger Bannister accomplished what everyone thought was unattainable. He ran the mile in three minutes, fifty-nine and four-tenths of a second, finally breaking the four-minute mile.

His feat ended a 70 plus year journey to push the limits of the human body. A goal that defied countless others for decades. Then 46 days later, John Landy, an Australian runner, not only broke the barrier again, he did so with a time of 3 minutes 58 seconds, breaking Bannister's record. One year later, three runners broke the four-minute barrier in a single race. Over the last half century, more than a thousand runners have achieved the feat once thought to be unattainable.

While the story is riveting to any sports enthusiast, it carries within it a much more useful lesson. Consider that all the best minds in the sports world worked on the strategy to get the first athlete past the four-minute threshold. They all turned out to be wrong. All the best athletes tried to use their superior conditioning and athletic abilities to overcome the barrier, but none of them could achieve what everyone believed to be impossible. How much of their struggle was psychological rather than physiological?

Very little changed in the capacity of the human body over that 70-year span. Not much changed in the physical condition of their environment or equipment either. What changed after Bannister, however, was the psychological state of those taking on the challenge. Overnight, they literally went from trying to achieve the impossible to attempting to better the possible. You can never truly underestimate the power of the mind, and the barriers erected by limiting beliefs.

According to Tony Robbins:

"Limiting beliefs are the stories we tell ourselves about who we are that hold us back from becoming who we are meant to be... They are often subconscious... We seek certainty in our routines, relationships and jobs. We're often averse to risk and don't want to get out of our comfort zones... When we don't

*believe we can get results… we give up before we start. We
don't put in our full effort. We sabotage our own success.
That's the very definition of limiting beliefs."*

How often do your limiting beliefs get in the way of your
potential success? Here are some strategies to help you
get out of your own way, according to Forbes Magazine.

Increase your emotional intelligence:
Increasing your emotional intelligence can raise your
awareness of your circumstances and your
understanding of yourself and others, and it can improve
your ability to act in your own best interests, as well as
the best interests of those around you.

Replace a limiting belief with an empowering belief:
Positive and accurate beliefs that support your life goals
can create a healthier mental state from which to work on
your goals.

Acknowledge that your beliefs are not facts:
As previously stated, they may feel true, but all they are
is a point of view — an often-mistaken point of view.

All of this is easier said than done, but if we don't get rid
of the limiting beliefs that hold us back, everything seems
impossible to achieve. I am a sports enthusiast, but the
real reason I love the Roger Bannister story is because it

inspires me to take on the things I'm told are impossible, with a willingness to fail forward, get up, dust myself off and try again. The alternative is just plain unacceptable to me. How about you?

Learning About Leadership from Unexpected Sources

Published by Seeking Veritas on Substack: Nov 28, 2023

On the subject of dogs, I am biased. To say otherwise would be a bold-faced lie. In all honesty, I often prefer the company of dogs to other humans. I find dogs provide an authentic experience that is extremely hard to get with their biped counterparts. Nonetheless, depending on your motivation, there is a lot that may be gleaned from observing them and their system of learning and behaving.

In my opinion, a relationship with a dog is about the purest thing you will find in this world. They start each day fresh and love you unconditionally; very few other sentient beings will offer you something with so few strings attached. If you are fair and kind to them, they will return it to you a hundred-fold, more than you deserve sometimes.

They don't care how smart you are, how rich you are, or how much you have achieved. They do not care about your titles, your net worth, what kind of home you have, or what type of car is in the driveway. They will love you when you are rich and can buy them the best cuts of meat. They will love you when you have nothing and still share your sandwich with them. Status signalling is completely irrelevant to a dog.

They are the greatest listeners, the best secret keepers, the most patient and the most loving companions. They will nuzzle you when you are sad, happy, lonely, or joyous; they are pure in a way that humans have forgotten how to be. Treat them with respect and they will defend you with their life. Abuse them and they will still love you, so NEVER take advantage of the greater humanity they often demonstrate.

You are never alone with a dog by your side, by your feet, or in your lap. They enable quiet self-reflection. allowing you to speak while they attend to the emotions you emit. Dogs are natural problem solvers; they observe their environment and pick up on the subtlest of cues to comprehend the best way for them to survive and thrive. I grant you that they are opportunity sensitive little creatures.

Dogs look for patterns, read physical cues, perhaps exploit emotional states from time to time, and are always observant and situationally aware. Their capacity to learn, transfer, and apply fascinates me. They provide us with an excellent opportunity to analyze how learning occurs, what motivates it, how it can be structured, and equally importantly, how it can be corrupted.

I combine my passion for teaching with my love for dogs. I make a living being an educator, I offer social commentary in my roles as a newspaper columnist and social commentator, but I find real joy in my weekend hobby work as a dog trainer.

I began training dogs as the COVID-19 pandemic lockdowns were winding down. Two services related to dogs were in high demand after the pandemic: shelters for abandoned dogs and training for untrained dogs. Some people put the time, effort, and money out to help their animals become better K9 citizens; the rest moved on to the next trendy social pastime. A reminder that mastery takes practice, and practice takes commitment.

For me, this all comes together in a logical way. As a dog trainer I analyze rudimentary behaviours based on evolutionary predispositions and conditioning; as a social commentator, I observe human interactions, communications, and social norms; and as an educator, I seek to inform perspectives and enhance the repertoire of transferable knowledge and skills for the people I work with.

I've commented before about my three principles for effective management, namely:

1. Consistency of application.
2. Clarity in communication.
3. Diligence in managing risk.

Funny how they apply as much to dog training as they do to management of human beings!

The Trick is Avoiding the Third Bite

Published by Seeking Veritas on Substack: Nov 29, 2023

If I had to identify the lessons, I walked away with thanks to my German Shepherd partners in the K-9 unit, I could probably fill a book. Here are a few of the lessons that I think are transferable to life in general, but ones I credit to the dogs who have passed through my life.

- Enter situations without preconceived ideas. It frees you to experience and become receptive to new and novel experiences.

95

- Pay attention to body language, it is far more accurate than words. Any time the verbal and non-verbals are incongruous, the non-verbals will serve as a barometer for the truth.
- Socialization is key, but most people get it wrong. The trick is learning to be neutral to new situations and environments so you can function anywhere. Being reactive to everything in your environment is both exhausting and dangerous.
- Praise and corrections are both essential to development. Keeping them balanced is the key to success.
- Respect is key; just because you can, doesn't always mean you should. Think about the bite force pressure of dog; now think about all the times they choose not to bite you.
- Kindness begets kindness and that is how relationships are built. Loyalty is rare in this world so cherish it when you find it.

The best things in life always last a short time; appreciate them and find healthy ways to keep moving forward. The first bite you experience is usually because you have no idea what you're doing. The second bite usually comes years later, usually a direct result of hubris and overconfidence. The trick to life is not getting bitten a third time.

My Introduction to Working Dogs

I do not have an inspiring story about how I was raised around dogs. I cannot tell you that they have always been a part of my life or that I always knew I would train dogs. Hell, I cannot even tell that you I presently make a living being a dog trainer.

All that sounds fantastic and makes for a great sales pitch, but it would be categorically untrue. Don't get me wrong, I wish I had a great story to share, one that had the making of the next great Togo or Hatchi movies. There are no iconic photographs reminiscent of Cesar Milan's childhood, of me walking down the street with dozens of dogs following me around. When I think back now it is hard to even remember a single dog from my childhood.

Owning a dog, even as a pet, never crossed my mind at any point in young adulthood. I was a young man with aspirations to be a police officer. I was working as a security guard; on my days off I would attend every police recruiting event on College Street in Toronto, the site of the police headquarters for what was then called the Metropolitan Toronto Police Force.

It was there that I learned that my two cornea transplant surgeries in childhood would render my uncorrected vision below the minimum standard to be a police

constable in Canada. With my future uncertain I would
have to find a new career path.

Sometimes in life adversity opens us up to new
possibilities. It gives us a reason to explore roads we
might have otherwise not travelled. While I was figuring
out my life options, I carried on working in the security
industry. Unsatisfied and longing for new opportunities,
I was open to explore just about anything back then to
get out of the mental rut I had found myself in.
I was sitting around the office one evening before my
shift and I saw a poster in our staff room. It read:

**Do you want to be a part of the K9 unit? Visit the K9
training academy and apply for a spot on our next
training course. Only a select few are accepted to the
program, so apply today and see if you have what it
takes to be a K9 Handler.**

So naturally, like any person who had no experience with
dogs or even rudimentary knowledge about working
dogs, I thought why not, this could be interesting! Most
people I share this story with now, think I was
completely nuts. I don't often argue the point! But I did
sign up and I did show up to the training facility on
Reesor Road in Scarborough, Ontario. That is where my
journey with dogs began.

As I pulled up the gravel driveway, I could hear the dogs barking, loud deep barks, something that had to be coming from very large dogs I imagined; scary some would say. Many of the other new trainees told me later that they judged the sound to be positively terrifying. At least one new trainee applicant never got out of his car. He sat there for five to seven minutes and then backed his car out and left. When I met him around the office later, he told me he knew in that moment K9 training was not for him.

I walked into the training facility, a large rectangular room with majestic and slightly vicious looking dog posters decorating the walls, along with pictures of previous cohorts. There was a distinct odour of cleaning products and wet dog, a scent that has probably become one with the building over the years.

There were only five new trainees in the class, the sixth having left before getting out of his car. We were instructed to stand in the middle of the room and told the instructor would be out shortly. I imagined a drill sergeant looking man, imposing in stature, flanked by mighty war dogs emerging from the doors at the end of the training room. I really had no idea what to expect, but any preconceived notions I may have had coming in were forever altered that day.

Eyes That Command Respect

A slight man entered the room. He couldn't have been more than 5'9", slender but athletic, probably in his mid-fifties with greying hair and kind eyes, the type that seemed to command respect. He wore the standard issue navy blue tactical pants (I think we called them tactical pants because it made us feel cool; if they were khaki in colour most other people would have just called them cargo pants!), and a black golf shirt with K9 embroidered on the left side of his chest.

As he walked over, I was surprised that he did not have a dog by his side. He also didn't look like he just jumped out of a Rambo movie. So, all my preconceived notions went out the window inside of thirty seconds. After brief pleasantries, he threw out a series of questions to the group:

Who owns a dog? Who has trained their own dogs? Who would call themselves a dog lover? And who feels confident that they will leave this program with these K9 Tags on their collar (gesturing to beautiful shiny collar pins that he had pulled out of his pocket)?

As expected, my four other colleagues all replied that they had dogs and loved dogs. Two of them stated they trained their own dogs, one said his family did so together, and the last guy reported having hired a trainer to help his dog.

The instructor looked over at me. I hadn't answered any of the questions; I also probably looked liked the least engaged person in the room. "So, what's your story?" he asked without any observable concern. "Well, I have never owned a dog or really been around them much and I don't know anything about dog training," was my reply. He did not flinch, he didn't even look shocked, he just calmly asked, "Confident you will be wearing the pins someday?" I shrugged. "Ask me in a couple of days," I replied. He smiled and moved on from the conversation.

I would graduate, I would wear the pins, and I would work twelve-hour shifts with a trained K9 always by my side. During my tenure in the unit, I worked primarily with two German Shepherd Dogs. The first a male King Shepherd specializing in protection work, and the second a female Shepherd specializing in detection. My time with those two dogs set me up for a successful career in the private sector for almost a decade before I moved over to academia.

The lessons I took away gave me the foundational knowledge, skills, and attitude for leadership. Skills I would require as I advanced to become one of the youngest managers in the company. My last position prior to becoming a professor was Senior Manager of Staffing & Development for the Toronto branch; we had 1400 employees and provided 40,000 hours of client services weekly.

The lessons made me a better communicator, a better reader of body language, tone and environment, and I firmly believe it made me a fairer and more objective person. Well, a person with a GSD bias, but who can really blame me for that!

Celebrating Shared Values Across Faiths and Traditions

Published by Seeking Veritas on Substack: Nov 7, 2023

In a time marked by complex challenges and growing polarization in our communities, I would like to contribute to an environment where differences are celebrated, where more people feel comfortable enough to join the conversation, and where we unite in our common humanity.

I turned to a source of profound wisdom and guidance: the diverse value systems of the world's belief traditions. Our world is a tapestry of cultures, faiths, and philosophies, each with its unique values and principles. At first glance, these belief systems may seem vastly distinct, but a closer examination reveals a shared foundation of virtues that can guide us toward a more harmonious and inclusive future.

I invite you to explore the remarkable commonalities that exist among major traditional values from different faiths and philosophies through a Kantian lens. Immanuel Kant (1724–1804) is a central figure in modern philosophy. He synthesized early modern rationalism and empiricism.

I started by digging up some common values shared by eleven systems of knowledge. They are based on the specific systems quoted below (I did not do a deep dive, just a quick review of values).

Belief Systems, Values and Principles:

> - Indigenous: Love, Respect, Courage, Truth, Honesty, Humility, Wisdom.
> - Hindu: Truth, Right Conduct, Love, Peace, Non-Violence.
> - Jewish: Life, Peace, Justice, Mercy, Scholarship, Sincerity of Intention.

- Muslim: Bravery, Consideration, Experience, Fairness, Justice, Honesty, Pursuit of Knowledge.
- Christian: Love, Joy, Peace, Forbearance (Tolerance/Patience), Kindness, Goodness, Faithfulness, Gentleness, Self-Control.
- Buddhist: Wisdom, Kindness, Patience, Generosity, Compassion.
- Sikh: Equality, Social Justice, Service to Humanity, Tolerance for other religions.
- Zoroastrian: Honesty, Charity, Love, Moderation without expecting praise or reward.
- Kantian: Respect for the humanity in others; acting in accordance with rules that could hold for everyone.
- Aristotelian: Prudence (Wisdom), Justice, Temperance, Courage.
- Wiccan: Do no harm, Mirth (Happiness), Reverence (Respect), Honour, Humility, Strength, Beauty, Power, Compassion.

From a Kantian perspective, the values outlined in these diverse traditions can be evaluated through the lens of the categorical imperative, which asserts that one should act only according to principles that could be applied universally. By analyzing these values through a Kantian framework, we can recognize how many ethical principles across traditions converge with the universalizability criterion. This approach emphasizes shared principles and a commitment to treating others with the same dignity and respect that we expect for ourselves.

I combined them and produced a list of foundational principles that can serve as the common ground for reducing social polarization and fostering cultural competence.

Foundational principles distilled from the values of major faith and traditional teachings:

1. Love and Compassion: Prioritize love and compassion in all interactions and decisions.
2. Power and Responsibility: Recognize the responsibility that comes with power and influence.
3. Justice and Fairness: Advocate for justice and fairness, ensuring equal treatment for all.
4. Wisdom and Knowledge: Seek wisdom and knowledge for informed decision-making.
5. Prudence and Restraint: Develop the capacity to govern your actions with restraint.
6. Kindness and Patience: Practice tolerance and understanding.
7. Generosity and Charity: Embrace generosity and charity to support those in need.
8. Truth and Honesty: Uphold truth and honesty as guiding principles for integrity.

9. Service to Humanity: Commit to service to humanity for the greater good.

10. Respect and Reverence: Show respect and reverence for the uniqueness of individuals and cultures.

11. Courage and Strength: Demonstrate courage and inner strength in overcoming challenges.

12. Humility and Modesty: Embrace humility and modesty, acknowledging our interconnectedness.

13. Sincerity and Integrity: Act with sincerity and integrity, fostering trust and transparency.

14. Gentleness: Foster respect and empathy.

15. Self-Control and Self-Improvement: Exercise self-control and commit to self-improvement.

16. Peace and Non-Violence: Promote peace and non-violence as fundamental values for conflict resolution.

17. Joy: Acknowledge the importance of happiness.

The promotion of dialogue and understanding among traditions may be viewed as a moral duty based on a Kantian analysis of today's world. It may serve as the common ground for reducing social polarization and fostering cultural competence between different belief systems, demonstrating the rich tapestry of common values that unite us all. Recognizing common ground allows us the opportunity to celebrate viewpoint diversity, and work towards reducing social polarization.

By embracing the common values that unite us and evaluating them through the lens of the categorical imperative, we can reduce social polarization and move towards a more inclusive society. A society that is built on the principles of universal ethics and moral duty, where diversity is a source of strength and inclusion, rather than a fault line along which we divide society up into innumerable sub-groups.

Section 2
POLITICS, POLICY, AND SOCIETY

Summary

We acknowledge that politics affect the realities of everyday life. From the corridors of power to grassroots movements, political decisions and public policies determine how resources are distributed, rights are upheld, and communities thrive—or struggle. This series of articles explores the dynamic interplay between these elements, dissecting how policy decisions influence social structures and how societal needs, in turn, shape political agendas.

With a focus on both historical context and contemporary issues, Politics, Policy, and Society aims to bridge the gap between theory and lived experience, offering a comprehensive understanding of the forces that govern our collective lives. Unpacking policies that underpin our lives and the political processes that bring them into existence is not a task for fainthearted, but it is one worth doing.

Freedom Fighter or Terrorist?

Published by Seeking Veritas on Substack: Jul 4, 2023

In 1948, Al Ednam Abidam was an active and vocal political dissenter. He strongly disagreed with the policies of his government and vehemently opposed the laws of his country. His early work as an activist was largely non-violent and consisted of organizing strikes and protests. However, the government did not take kindly to the political and civil unrest he was creating. This resulted in his first arrest for treason in 1956.

In the years that followed, critical interactions between the government and the population led Abidam to become disheartened and pessimistic about the possibility that peaceful protest could achieve the goals he and others like him were working for. They felt that non-violent measures would not and could not provide the catalyst for change they so desperately yearned for.

In 1961, they formed an underground militant organization called MK and named Abidam as commander-in-chief. Under his leadership, they developed strategies they felt would create sufficient disruption to destabilize the government and the laws of the land. They felt like they had no other options since they could not get their voice heard through recognized channels. MK launched bombing attacks on government targets and coordinated planning for guerrilla warfare directed against their own government.

In 1963, following a raid on MK's organizational hideout, law enforcement found documents for future attacks and warfare tactics. Abidam, along with eleven other MK leaders, were arrested and charged under the Sabotage Act. He admitted to many of the charges, but strongly defended his use of violence. Despite his impassioned defence — arguments that sought to demonstrate the justification for his actions and place them in the social context he perceived — he was found guilty of four charges of sabotage and sentenced to life imprisonment.

In 1985, the President of his country offered to release him from jail if he renounced violence, but Abidam refused and declined the offer for release on those conditions.

In 1989, his country had a newly elected president, and with the changing political attitudes of the time, the President decided to release him from jail given he was now 71 years old. The decision was not universally celebrated, and while there was support to release him based on his time served, others objected given that the US Defence Department listed his organization among fifty-two of the "world's more notorious terrorist groups."

Within three years of his release from jail however, he reassumed leadership of his organization. Al Ednam Abidam remained on the US Terrorist watch list until 2008 when he was 90 years old. This time under his leadership, the organization was managed differently, and he made many strides towards realizing the goals he had set out to achieve in his early days as an activist. The work he did was well received by the international community and his story found a more receptive audience in the 1990s. In fact, the political and social tides in the global community had changed so much that he was awarded a Nobel Peace Prize in 1993, a major accomplishment for a previously convicted terrorist who was still actively listed on the US Terrorist watch list.

One could argue that this was the ultimate example of changing social attitudes and forgiveness, and the emergence of a new world that had a different set of morals and values from the one in which he was convicted and sent to jail for crimes he admitted to committing. With his renewed public appeal and support, his organization was able to mobilize politically becoming a recognized political party in his country. They had won so much public support that his party ultimately emerged victorious in the presidential elections of 1994, resulting in Al Ednam Abidam becoming the new President of the country.

The facts of the story above are completely true and not embellished for dramatic effect; it is in the historical record and is studied in classrooms around the world. It forces us to examine our views on political dissent and challenges the notion that we should always trust our government and our laws.

The story illustrates the famous quote by Frédéric Bastiat:

"When law and morality contradict each other, the citizen has the cruel alternative of either losing his moral sense or losing his respect for the law."

It forces us to question what we should do if we have tried every legal avenue to address our perceived injustices, but they fall upon deaf ears. Do we take the law into our own hands? Do we rely on the notion that time and tides will change the public view? Do we trust that notion presented by Martin Luther King Jr., that the moral arc of the universe is long but always bends towards justice? Or, perhaps we should act on the principle put forth by the great and venerated American founding father, Thomas Jefferson, who eloquently stated:

"If a law is unjust, a man is not only right to disobey it, he is obligated to do so."

In this context do we view the historical actions of Al Ednam Abidam as one of a freedom fighter or a terrorist?

What if I now admit that I spelled his name backwards, and the person whose story I have been retelling is none other than Madiba, the African root name by which his people refer to him, instead of his English name Mandela. Does knowing the name change your entire perception of the story? How much did the imagery

influence your thoughts? Can you articulate the
difference between a freedom fighter and a terrorist?

Unfriendly Fire: The Terror of War

Published by Seeking Veritas on Substack: Jul 25, 2023

"I am not a victim of war anymore. I am a survivor… I am so thankful that all social media all over the world is just talking about my picture. I think that is so powerful. We have to have the truth. The story has to be told. To show people what happened." – Kim Phúc Phan Thi, 2022

Why do we call it "friendly fire"? There is nothing friendly about it. On June 8, 1972, Kim Phúc Phan Thi was nine years old. She lived in the village of Trang Bang northwest of Saigon, now called Ho Chi Minh City.

117

Along with other members of her family, she had been sheltering at a nearby temple. North Vietnamese forces had occupied their village. Mistakenly believing they had spotted enemy soldiers fleeing, a South Vietnamese air force pilot "flying in at around 2,000 feet and 500 mph, had seconds to identify the group... assumed that the group were armed North Vietnamese Army, and so he dropped his ordnance on their position." Two of Kim Phúc's cousins were killed, along with several of South Vietnam's own people. A terrible mistake commonly referred to as friendly fire.

In a 2022 interview with CBC producer Sylvia Thomson, Kim Phúc recalled:

"As soon as the napalm touched me, the clothes burned off. I still remember my arm and seeing all the fire. I was so terrified, and I was so scared. And I thanked God my feet weren't burned, and I was able to run out of that fire.... We just kept running and running and running for a while ... and I cried out 'Too hot! Too hot!' The soldiers tried to help me. They tried to pour the water over me, and at that moment, I lost consciousness."

The now iconic picture was captured by a then 21-year-old Vietnamese-American photographer named Nick Ut for the Associated Press. On seeing her suffering, Nick helped her and other survivors to a hospital. Burns covered roughly 50 percent of her body, and her odds of survival were considered extremely low. Over the next 14 months, Phúc received 17 surgeries, but she was left with serious restrictions in her range of movement that would last for a decade until receiving reconstructive surgery in West Germany in 1982. The picture was officially titled "The Terror of War" but has informally been referred to as "Napalm Girl" ever since. It received a Pulitzer Prize, recognition for the function of journalism in shedding light on the terror inherent in war. Kim Phúc and Nick Ut keep in contact to this day more than 50 years later.

According to a CNN article by Oscar Holland, Kim Phúc had dreamed about becoming a doctor. However, the Vietnamese government removed her from medical school to use her in propaganda campaigns. She initially hated the photograph and struggled with all the attention. The government eventually allowed her to study in Havana Cuba, where she met her now husband, Bui Huy Toan. The couple married in 1992.

While on route to their honeymoon in Moscow, their plane stopped over to refuel in Gander, Newfoundland. The couple left the international transit area and asked the Canadian government for political asylum. In 1997 they became Canadian citizens. The couple now live in Ajax, Ontario.

When asked how she felt about her picture being shared around the world and about all the interviews, Kim replied:

"I am not a victim of war anymore. I am a survivor. I feel like 50 years ago, I was a victim of war but 50 years later, I was a friend, a helper, a mother, a grandmother and a survivor calling out for peace. And I work to fulfil my dream to give back to children who are victims of war. I am so thankful that all social media all over the world is just talking about my picture. I think that is so powerful. We have to have the truth. The story has to be told. To show people what happened."

She founded the Kim Foundation International, which provides aid to child victims of war. Her road from Saigon to Ajax was paved with pain but also forgiveness.

The fact that she now lives in a town less than 15 minutes away from me is a stark reminder that behind every iconic photo lies a real person, whose life is complex and multidimensional; whose whole story is worth knowing and retelling — so that lessons from history do not wither and fade from our collective memory.

Civility, Hyperbole & Democracy

Published by Seeking Veritas on Substack: Jul 14, 2024

On July 13, 2024, former US President Donald Trump narrowly survived an assassination attempt at a presidential campaign event. He becomes the third American President to have suffered an injury resulting from an unsuccessful attempt, along with Theodore Roosevelt in 1912, and Ronald Reagan in 1981. Four sitting US Presidents have been killed: Abraham Lincoln in 1865, James A. Garfield in 1881, William McKinley in 1901, and John F. Kennedy in 1963. In every one of these incidents, notwithstanding the physical and psychological impact to the actual human holding the office, the greatest harm inflicted was to civility and democracy.

When hyperbole polarizes a society and fills people with so much rage and hatred for the "other" side, we lose the greater value and purpose of democracy itself. It may not seem self-evident in the age of social media (where political elections more closely resemble WWE Grudge Matches rather than a competition for ideas), but democracy is rooted in compromise and respect for the collective voice. It is meant to be a competition for the best ideas as agreed upon by vote, the antidote to monarchy and authoritarianism, the guard rail against totalitarianism.

Polarization depends on our capacity to remain abstract in our vitriol. When political parties get entrenched in tribalism, greater energy is expended voting out our adversaries rather than voting in the best options. The point of opposition is to allow dissent and meaningful discourse to elevate the value of all our policies, to come together in the end to create more inclusive governance that better serves the people. When the vote doesn't go our way, we get to try again at the next election.

The current political climate has devolved into an "us versus them" binary, a zero-sum game that only leads to a race to the bottom. Leaders and political operatives who peddle in hate mongering and fear contribute to the erosion of civility. Hyperbole makes for great clickbait but fails to provide meaningful political change. The practice of "othering" our political opponents needs to stop so sensible discourse about actual issues can occur. We cannot rely solely on political leaders to make these changes; everyone has a part. An informed citizenry is the strongest foundation upon which to build an effective democracy.

I don't agree with much of Trump's policy positions, I dislike his general modus operandi and detest his willingness to erode the professionalism of public office, but attempting to assassinate him is not the answer. That act of violence itself is an affront to democracy, an insult to every voting member of that nation who does their part in securing a better future for their country by casting a ballot instead of a bullet.

Unfortunately, this heinous attempt on Trump's life, regardless of what we think of him as a person, is more likely to embolden the already polarized masses. Where a lesson could be learned about extremes, I fear it will be a rallying cry to double down. The image of his bloodied face and arm held up in defiance will make for an effective political statement that fires up his base and quite possibly swings the election in his favour. Whether or not he gets re-elected should not detract from our collective need to reduce polarization.

Today is a good day to remember the character of a former US presidential candidate, the late John McCain. In the face of vitriolic hate and misinformation directed against his political opponent, he demonstrated civility and a commitment to democracy.

When McCain encountered a voter he could confidently count in his column, who suggested Obama was an Arab who couldn't be trusted, he took the microphone back and calmly reminded her that she was wrong; that his opponent was a decent family man, a fellow citizen, even if they disagreed on the fundamentals of how to govern. That should be the standard of class and civility. It was a masterclass in rejecting hyperbole and showing respect for those we disagree with.

Our children will be the beneficiaries of a better world if all of us commit to turning down the volume on rhetorical nonsense and demonstrate civility toward those we disagree with. Our children need to see us say violence is not the answer and does little to create lasting social change; the ballot box is where they will one day make themselves heard.

PS: Donald J Trump won the American presidency four months later.

The Forest and The Trees

Published by Seeking Veritas on Substack: Jun 4, 2023

"He is not my Prime Minister!" the man shouted, his face flushed, eyes narrowed, and lips pursed. His comment was clearly personal, not some passing remark made between mates at the local pub. It caught my attention right away; I was sitting two tables away from those men. As I looked up from the plate in front of me and peered over at them, my first thought, I'm afraid to confess, was highly prejudiced. I wondered who this ignorant lowbrow was and why he was yelling in a family restaurant. In all fairness, the pub was only separated from the dining area by plants and a half wall. I suppose it's easy to think that was a sufficient barrier to demarcate the kid-friendly area from where the adult conversations happen.

"Not my Prime Minister/President" is a phrase I've heard many times in recent years, yet the oddity of the statement never ceases to annoy me — sorry, intrigue me. I wanted to walk over and ask the man to explain whose Prime Minister he was exactly? I'm not sure that question would have prompted a well thought-out or even a logical answer. But perhaps this was the product of my own biases. I see those who understand and those who don't, conservatives and liberals, good and evil people, the enlightened and the dullards, the givers and takers, the accomplished and the entitled. In short, us and them. Do I actually see them, or is polarization so ubiquitous that I simply feel compelled to think in those terms? Are those men equally compelled and indoctrinated? Is this simply the state of our society?

Much figurative ink has been spilled writing about polarization in our society. Some believe it was the 43rd American President, George W. Bush, who revived the sentiment. To be sure, he made a dent on the world when he famously said on the 20th of September 2001, "Every nation, in every region, now has a decision to make. Either you are with us, or you are with the terrorists." As far as speeches go, it was neat, concise, deliberate, and purposeful. And from a social psychology perspective, it was a brilliantly simple choice: angel or devil, righteous or evil, freedom fighter or terrorist. A simple binary, us or them. And, of course, it works all the better if we ignore the false dilemma in the argument, ignoring any other possible alternative.

But let us not get hung up on the details. Polarization depends on our capacity to remain abstract in our vitriol. After all, Bush did have bi-partisan support and applause when he delivered that speech. That night, he promised the United States was a country awakened to danger and called to defend freedom. He described American grief as metamorphosed into anger, and that anger transformed into resolve. George W. Bush went on to promise, *"Whether we bring our enemies to justice, or bring justice to our enemies, justice will be done."* A promise that lived up to the now tried-and-tested political foreign policy of strategic ambiguity. Today no ambiguity is left; justice was served for the 2,977 victims who perished on September 11th, 2001, the single deadliest attack on American soil.

When the dust finally settled over the grey Manhattan sky, the 2,997 mostly civilian lives lost on September 11, 2001, would be avenged over the next twenty plus years. The so-called war on terror became the longest war in

American history, coming at an additional cost to American and allied military personnel. An estimated 2,298 US military troops, 1,145 allied troops, and approximately 3,900 US contractors would perish in the military response. If you are keeping score, though, the justice brought to the enemies would inflict approximately 156,000 deaths in Afghanistan and Pakistan, and an additional 249,000 deaths in Iraq, for a grand total of 405,000 people in three countries. Of those, according to the Watson Institute of International & Public Affairs at Brown University, approximately 280,000 were civilians. A lesson was definitely learned in the Middle East and surrounding regions.

The war on terror has been a permanent fixture in our Western psyche for over two decades. It has shaped our discourse and altered our perceptions. This is really the undercurrent that contextualized the pub conversation which prompted my pontification here. From the othering of people from far-away lands to the contemporary policy of North American immigration bringing mostly brown faces to its shores, there's a lot for us to unpack. The reality is our world is changing, the shades around us darkening, the culture shifting and, let's face it, that makes some people feel very uncomfortable. From these circumstances rise the perfect conditions to incubate tribalism and build up the walls, ideologically in some places and manifested differently in others. Those men did not like the politics of that effeminate head of state who did not represent them. He was undoubtedly an "other"!

The history of democracy goes all the way back to ancient world, from Sumer to India and from the Greeks to the Romans, all the way until its resurgence during the enlightenment. Yet after traversing this vast expanse of time and space, we seem to have lost the kernel that makes it worth maintaining. And we see this clearly when we hear people say, "I don't read non-fiction," "who has time for all that history stuff," and "live in the moment baby!" But what does this have to do with those two men in the pub? Well, as their conversation continued, and I couldn't help eavesdropping, they pulled out all the chart toppers: "Libtards," "commies," "turban-wearing politicians using TikTok as a platform," and "the 5% hijacked by those extremists who split the vote but do have somewhat of a point." That PM who represents those "others" who are not really Canadian makes it impossible to voice thoughts openly because freedom is being threatened; and also, the AR15 is an ideal choice for deer hunting, you know? Although if I'm being honest here, my favourite had to be the one about us only needing one party.

To be clear, the conversation could as easily have included commentary about country bumpkins colluding with the folks in the one percentile, or misogyny and the need to get woke, or the out-of-touch traditionalists of gender and white hegemony. Somehow all of it culminating in the need to have one, just one, party so no one had to deal with these holdouts from a by-gone era. I guess I'm saying that left or right, up or down, there is enough tribalism to go around. It turns out everyone is always right inside their echo chambers, surrounded by like-minded friends and allies. All fighting the clear and present danger lurking around the corner by the "others."

In reality, a quick TikTok-length tour through the history of just the 20th century would highlight the problems with the policy of One. From the one-child policy to the one-party system of governance, from the one great society to the one superior race to the one-drop rule. It might even provide some insight into the vilification of the evil other, those other-worldly mongrels who threaten our way of life, our culture, our traditions and our nationhood, the specifics of which, of course, are infinitely malleable to accommodate the zeitgeist of the times. Perhaps these Others have the wrong Holy Book or the wrong Holy Man, or maybe even the wrong Holy Spirit. Perhaps they possess the wholly wrong skin tone or the wholly wrong ancestry. Perhaps their ancestors were too heavily subjugated or too unevenly privileged, too high in the caste system or so low they are outside of it. All one needs to know is the self-evident truth that wherever there is an us, there is inevitably a "them," those others.

When our political parties get so tribal, we spend all our time voting out our adversaries rather than voting in the best options. It then becomes easy to lose the forest through the trees. The point of opposition is to allow dissent and meaningful discourse to elevate the value of all our policies, to come together in the end to create more inclusive governance that better serves all Canadians. Democracy is about compromise; it's about the collective voice. It is the antidote to monarchy and authoritarianism, the guard rail against totalitarianism. We could lose sight of the forest and focus on the individual trees, but this democratic state of ours only works if we have the courage to keep it.

Or, I don't know, we could just live in the moment baby!

Apolitical: Virtue or Vice

Published by Seeking Veritas on Substack: Aug 29, 2023

"Many forms of Government have been tried, and will be tried in this world of sin and woe. No one pretends that democracy is perfect or all-wise. Indeed, it has been said that democracy is the worst form of Government except for all those other forms that have been tried from time to time...." – Winston S Churchill, 11 November 1947

It is common for someone to claim that they are "apolitical" to signal their objectivity. Corporations make that claim even more loudly and proudly. Very few people question the implied logic behind the assertion that being apolitical is synonymous with being neutral or objective, arguably a virtue. Fewer still question whether the claim is merely convenient; undoubtedly a vice!

Within a democratic society, civic engagement and political participation form the foundation of our social contract. It is the mechanism by which we elect the government that represents us, protects our rights, and preserves our freedoms. It is the defining feature that differentiates a democracy from an autocracy, be it an oligarchy, dictatorship, or even a monarchy.

Democracy is necessarily messy. We put our favoured ideologies — social and economic — into the proverbial town square. We then agree by consensus, administered by vote, the policies and parties that govern us by consent for a fixed period of time. If our decision proves to be unsatisfactory, we return at the next opportunity and utilize our vote to make our voice heard. When the last ballot has been cast, the people have spoken; the campaigning is over, and we are meant to function as a unified society.

Once government is formed, the function of the opposition parties are equally critical to our democracy. They are the guardrails against excess. The push and pull of perspective are meant to bring us to middle ground that serves the best interests of all citizens. The political jostling is intended to produce balanced outcomes, necessary compromise, and social progress.

When you can no longer tell the difference between your attitude towards a sports rivalry and the "other" political party, something has gone terribly wrong!
It has been said that democracy is the worst type of government except for all the other alternatives. I submit that our democracy is not without its flaws and blind spots, but having lived in a country with an absolute authoritarian monarch previously, I assure you the flaws are worth the bargain.

Let's return to the debate about whether we should consider the apolitical claim a virtue or a vice. Here are some points for consideration before you decide:

1. Humans are tribal by nature, so neutrality is probably a myth... Everyone knows that humans are tribal and most assume we merely hide our preferences (some call these biases). So, who are we fooling?
2. Civic engagement is critical to the democratic process... so naturally we hide any indication that we participate in the democratic process.
3. We bemoan low voter turnout and constantly criticize the young for their unwillingness to engage

in local politics... so naturally we model that political affiliation is a trait that corrupts our ability to deal with others.

4. We teach children about government in elementary school. By high school, we educate them about the various political parties and discuss how they present different ideas about the best approach to governance. In post-secondary, we encourage them to run for student government and become informed about community activism... so naturally we follow all that with hiding political affiliation and use being apolitical as a measure of being objective. (Why didn't we trust the purpose of being informed?)

5. When we leave our country and travel abroad, we are all Canadians (or insert your country here)... so naturally at home we are red, blue, orange, or green — mortal enemies locked in eternal combat for the soul of the nation.

6. If one is genuinely apolitical, could that not also be symptomatic of an uninformed electorate or worse, an apathetic one?!

Differences in political perspective are what make a democracy, a democracy! Regardless of our political preferences, we need to collectively recommit ourselves to finding our common humanity and remembering our common national purpose. The "other" parties are not our enemies, they are merely fellow citizens with divergent views. We could take a note from Voltaire's poem, La Bégueule, and stop making perfection the enemy of the good.

Caught in the Crossfire: The Canadian Government vs. Social Media

Published by Seeking Veritas on Substack: Aug 15, 2023

"It's like Nineteen Eighty-Four. Who would ever have imagined that in Canada the federal government would pass laws banning people from effectively seeing the news?" – Conservative Leader Pierre Poilievre

In all the discussion about the Canadian Online News Act, Bill C-18, passed in June 2023, the focal point has been large scale tax avoidance and the impact to news

organizations in Canada. It almost appears like a battle between tech giants, big government, and large news corporations. But there are others caught in the crossfire who rarely get the attention but disproportionately suffer the impact.

Love it or hate it, social media has come to play a major role in our society. There is plenty to criticize on the internet, but it also offers significant advantage to many people who would struggle without the reach provided by the platforms.

Bill C-18 "requires big tech giants like Google and Meta to pay media outlets for news content they share or otherwise repurpose on their platforms." In response to the Bill, Meta, which owns Facebook and Instagram, has officially begun ending news availability on its platforms in Canada. "Canadians will no longer be able to view or post news content on Facebook or Instagram." Google also plans to remove links to local Canadian news content. Their global affairs president, Kent Walker, called the Online News Act "unworkable" and an "uncapped financial liability."

Lost in the discussion is the local level impact caused by this corporate game of chicken. "Police services across Canada are grappling with how they will relay emergency information, including breaking news and details of missing persons, once Meta begins permanently removing news from its social media platforms." The reality is that a great deal of people use social media to stay connected to their local community. Local infrastructure and communication models are heavily dependent on these platforms to disseminate critical information in a timely manner.

The large news corporations have the financial capacity to develop, market and launch their own apps. But even that is not the best solution to the problem. News was once considered a social good, not merely a consumer product. By moving news to individual platforms, we are more likely to unintentionally increase polarization by fragmenting the pool of available information.

As reported in the New York Times, "The Canadian bill is modeled after a 2021 law passed in Australia, the first country to enact such legislation. At the time, Meta temporarily blocked sharing news links in Australia, before coming to a deal and lifting the ban." Former heritage minister Pablo Rodriguez said he hoped the Liberal government could negotiate a similar agreement with Meta. But the Australian law was different because it allowed the company to negotiate private deals with publishers outside of the framework of the regulations. Bill C-18 does not.

Local news, opinion editorials, community safety stories, and coverage of local politics have a major influence on community health and integration. People may still download a free news app; some may even subscribe to a news outlet for full access to all their digital content, but most won't -— and the majority that do subscribe will utilize a limited number of news sources, thereby reducing their exposure to divergent viewpoints.

For all its ills, social media created a marketplace of ideas. Much like real societies, it is a messy marketplace complete with contradictions, conflicts, and actors with bad intent. But, outside of some utopian ideal, those features exist in every society, real and virtual. One could argue they are a characteristic of the human condition.

Conflicting views, divergent thinking, and varied perspectives are all central features of a healthy democracy. Perhaps more than just the corporate giants and government actors, we should also consider the impact to local communities caught in the crossfire and likely to become collateral damage in the feud.

Ford's Ontario Government Labour Announcements

Published by Seeking Veritas on Substack: Jul 19, 2023

The Ford government has been actively shoring up support by appealing to voters concerned about employment and the economy. Three recent policy decisions have been publicized within the last three months, receiving mixed reviews from the public. They include announcements about changes to the apprenticeship pathway for the skilled trades, entry requirements for new policing applicants, and the removal of "Canadian experience requirements" for internationally trained engineers. Here is a quick scorecard to evaluate them together.

In early March, the government announced that they will allow students, starting in Grade 11, to transition to full-time apprenticeship programs while still earning a high school diploma. The move was intended to address the labour shortages given the province's stated intention to build 1.5 million new homes by 2031.

However, the government did not appear to have a clear plan to ensure that those students entering apprenticeship programs prior to completing high school would actually graduate with a secondary school diploma. This may not seem like a significant problem until one considers the 37% attrition rate in the sector. Some of that turnover is positive — promotions, business ventures, etc. — but a lot of it is tied to injuries caused by stress on the body, pressure related to the seasonal nature of work, and social stigma on the quality of the occupation. Many people who subsequently leave the trades would find themselves ill prepared to transition to other careers in the economy if their highest level of completed education would render them generally unemployable in the broader labour market.

The government followed the skilled trades announcement with a second labour related one in April, this one addressing police recruitment challenges. Premier Ford announced that the government would boost lagging police recruitment by eliminating the post-secondary education requirement for new police applicants. In a previous article, I have argued that the move ignores research and previous recommendations from the police themselves. It appears like a short-term solution to a recruitment challenge, but one with significant downstream effects that could adversely impact community safety, public trust, and the mental health of future police officers themselves.

The labour announcement in May was related to the licensing requirements for engineers in Ontario. A vast majority of internationally trained professionals find themselves underemployed despite having the technical proficiency required for jobs they are educated to undertake. Labour Minister Monte McNaughton has stated that the regulatory bodies have until December 2nd, 2023, to remove the Canadian work experience requirement from the licensing process or face fines upwards of $100,000. The Professional Engineers Ontario (PEO) led the way by becoming the first professional regulatory body to remove the requirement from their application criteria.

The decision removes a barrier to licensing, allowing new immigrants to seek economic integration more efficiently.

The licensing requirements do not lower the competence threshold and maintains the rigorous standards ensuring only properly qualified individuals practice engineering in Ontario. New immigrants, especially internationally trained professionals, do not expect a lowering of the standards, but rather a fair and equitable pathway to entry. The move makes sense given our focus on attracting professionals to immigrate and contribute to Canada's economic growth.

On balance, the engineering announcement is a positive step that promotes economic and social integration for new immigrants with international experience and education. It also creates a positive precedent from which to evaluate other regulatory requirements. The policing announcement may be judged fairly as negative, given it does little to actually address recruitment challenges; and may create a myriad of downstream problems. Finally, the skilled trades announcement clearly needs some improvement. We do have a housing crisis and urgent action is required, but let's not do it at the expense of our essential workers trying to enter the trades.

The Unpredictability of Elections

Published by Seeking Veritas on Substack: Aug 22, 2023

"Talk is cheap, voting is free; take it to the polls."
– Nanette L. Avery

After ten years as the Member of Parliament for the Durham Riding, former Conservative Party leader Erin O'Toole decided to resign and vacate his seat. It opens the door to a by-election that will bring new representation to Ottawa.

A little history from Durham, Ontario

"Since its inception, Durham has been represented by the Conservative Party for 84 of 119 years."

The federal seat in Durham has been consistently held by a conservative candidate since 2004. In fact, dating back to 1904 when the electoral district was first contested, the Conservatives have faired significantly better than the Liberals in this riding. Since its inception, Durham has been represented by the Conservative Party for 84 of 119 years. That said, the next conservative candidate would be ill-advised to consider the riding a lock and should be prepared to appeal to an ever-shifting population demographic in the region. Likewise, left-leaning candidates would benefit from recognizing the diversity of viewpoints that exist among minority populations.

Appealing to the new voters in the region will be essential to securing their support. The riding of Milton, Ontario may offer an essential lesson in electoral unpredictability.

A lesson from Milton, Ontario

A federal redistribution took effect for Milton by the 2015 election which the Conservative Party won, but they have lost every subsequent election thereafter. In 2015, Lisa Raitt of the Conservative Party won the riding with 22,378 votes. In 2019, she secured an almost identical number of votes and still lost the riding by almost 9,000 votes to the Liberal Party candidate, Adam Van Koeverden. In the space of four years the number of eligible voters in Milton increased by 13,000. If Raitt secured the same voters she had in the previous election, it suggests that the Conservative Party was unable to grow their base in that riding. The failure to appeal to Milton's newest residents arguably cost the Conservative Party a federal seat, one they are yet to recover given Van Koeverden retained his seat in 2021 with an even larger margin over the next Conservative Party candidate, Nadeem Akbar.

The riding of Durham will experience a federal redistribution in 2024, with new boundaries and a new name. According to the 2021 Census, the population for Durham Region has increased significantly since 2016. All the municipalities in Durham (except Scugog) experienced population growth; the region's growth outpaced the neighbouring regions of York, Toronto, and Peel. Over 70% of Durham Region's population growth was through immigration. The similarities make Milton a relevant case study for that reason.

Learning from Milton
Giving consideration to the shifting demographics and the population growth in Durham, candidates will need to appeal to both long-standing and new residents of

Durham to ensure electoral success. Durham residents share a common humanity and a spirit of entrepreneurship that unites them as a community.

The Conservative Party needs to widen its base and appeal to new voters, including a younger demographic and immigrants. The Liberals and NDP cannot assume that minority voters are a lock. There is a diversity of thought and political ideology among immigrant communities; making the case to earn their vote is the minimum expectation.

When representing a diverse constituency, candidates do not need to pick between appealing to one demographic over another. Instead, they should focus on a politics of unity rather than division. Regardless of what the politicians do within their campaigns, for all us citizens out there, the process only truly works when we exercise our civic responsibilities and engage in the democratic process.

Neutrality: A Foundational Principle NOT a Policy of Convenience

Published by Seeking Veritas on Substack: Oct 17, 2023

"The neutrality of the university as an institution arises then not from a lack of courage nor out of indifference and insensitivity. It arises out of respect for free inquiry and the obligation to cherish a diversity of viewpoints."
– Kalven Committee: Report on the University's Role in Political and Social Action

Lessons from History

I'm not sure why we don't spend more time in primary, secondary, and post-secondary schooling teaching and learning history. So often those stories are almost perfectly analogous to some contemporary issue we are dealing with and could offer a blueprint for potential strategies we might consider.

During the 1960s, American society was contending with widespread escalating racial tension, a sexual revolution that sought to redefine traditional gender roles, and opposition protests against a perceived unjust war on the other side of the world. Any of that sound familiar? If I merely took the date out, would you be able to tell it apart from 2023?

Corporations, including colleges and universities have taken a beating in the media for positions they've expressed or refuse to express on current world events. Boards and senior leadership everywhere are spinning their wheels figuring out what kind of message they should be putting out, afraid that any comment is likely to incite anger with one of the many groups affected by current events. In a recent article by FIRE (Foundation for Individual Rights and Expression), the organization urged colleges and universities to adopt a position of institutional neutrality. The article utilized the principles outlined in the Kalven Report, commissioned in 1967 by the then president of the University of Chicago. Chaired by Harry Kalven, Jr., a leading First Amendment scholar, the committee produced a report containing recommendations on how the institution should approach political and social action.

"The mission of the university is the discovery, improvement, and dissemination of knowledge."

Scope Creep

The question leaders are grappling with surrounds what message they should be sending. I would argue that this is the wrong question in the first place, and one that sets everyone down a path that is highly problematic. The reason that post-secondary institutions are expected to take a stance on current geopolitical issues is because the sector has voluntarily engaged in social issues in the past. The drift towards virtue signalling and supporting the cause of the day has become almost common practice in North American corporations and on educational campuses. It is, however, the root of the problem, not a symptom of the operation. The core business of an academic institution is to provide education, disseminate knowledge, and prepare the workforce of the future. That purpose gets compromised when we drift outside our lane.

Binary thinking, which dominates our contemporary discourse, has taken up a disproportionate amount of airtime lately. It inaccurately reflects only the polar ends of the ideological spectrum, while ignoring the vast space in the middle, occupied by everyday people. It also abhors complexity and in so doing, takes a reductive approach to complex social issues.

"The instrument of dissent and criticism is the individual faculty member or the individual student. The university is the home and sponsor of critics; it is not itself the critic... To perform its mission in the society, a university must sustain an extraordinary environment of freedom of inquiry and maintain an independence from political fashions, passions, and pressures. A university, if it is to be true to its faith in intellectual inquiry, must embrace, be hospitable to, and encourage the widest diversity of views within its own community."

Vicarious Trauma

A common practice in many organizations is to point to some headline in the newspaper, express sorrow for the pain being felt by those encountering the newsworthy incident, and then link it to local communities far removed by alluding to vicarious trauma. Of course, everyone who may or may not have read that news story (a reasonable proposition given the decline in news readership) is offered wellness services.

Some people will argue that there is an arbitrary decision being made about which world events require messaging based on what is trending. Here is a simple idea: if wellness and awareness of resources is the goal, just regularly communicate the organization's commitment to wellness and availability of supports. I assure you that the minute you pick one headline, someone else will point to another. If you picked every headline in the National Post, someone is sure to ask why you didn't review the Globe & Mail. That's the nature of following trends, they just keep changing.

"It is a community but only for the limited, albeit great, purposes of teaching and research. It is not a club, it is not a trade association, it is not a lobby. Since the university is a community only for these limited and distinctive purposes, it is a community which cannot take collective action on the issues of the day without endangering the conditions for its existence and effectiveness."

Sustainable Governance

What is an organization to do in these confusing times of corporate citizenship? Perhaps focus on sustainable governance rather than virtue signalling. Remember that the institution houses the critics and revolutionaries; the institution shouldn't play that role. Step back for a moment, refresh your memory on why the institution exists, how it meets it objectives, and when it should just shut up!

Post-secondary institutions should steer clear of making moralistic pronouncements on social issues. Diverse staff and student bodies benefit more from:

1. Consistency of application.
2. Clarity of communication.
3. Judicious management of risk.

Rather than stack ranking marginalized communities (the evaluation of suffering and privilege is highly subjective and emotionally charged), focus on the removal of barriers to access and opportunity writ large. Rather than guarantees of equality of outcome focus on more universal principles like respect for others on campus. Rather than feeling the need to lobby a particular position, choose common humanity over immutable differences, and common cause rather than common enemy as your guiding principle.

Accept that intellectual inquiry is messy, but necessary. Most of all, model restraint; facts move and shift as situations unfold and life rarely, if ever, is made of wholly right or wholly wrong perspectives. Make no mistake, neutrality is neither easy nor comfortable, but it is a principle worthy of consideration and deliberation.

As the Kalven Report so adroitly highlights, the neutrality of an institution does not signal a lack of courage nor indifference and insensitivity. It opts consciously and deliberately for neutrality out of respect for free inquiry and the obligation to cherish a diversity of viewpoints.

Technologically Enabled Dissent

Published by Seeking Veritas on Substack: Jul 11, 2023

"In a room where people unanimously maintain a conspiracy of silence, one word of truth sounds like a pistol shot."
– Czesław Miłosz

In our modern, technologically driven, and knowledge based global society, we have arguably greater access to information and data than at any other time in human history. One would imagine that given all this information that is readily and freely accessible, we would be the most informed civilization that has ever inhabited this planet. That may be objectively true, but how have we mobilized this knowledge?

The vast amounts of data consumed on a daily basis, and the copious amounts of data available, have arguably convoluted our ability to discern quality information that is reliable and valid from that which is clickbait, or downright false. Equally troubling is the concept of personalized news and media feeds that utilize algorithms to predict what we would like to read or consume. The result is an altered sense of reality; an existence inside an echo chamber that reiterates our own views and reflects only our own preferences. Personally curated content simultaneously limits the flow of alternative perspectives that may enlighten or inform our perspectives — albeit at the cost of emotional or intellectual comfort.

All this shielding from discomfort, and reinforcement of what we already accept, has a chilling effect on objective discourse and is better suited to polarize, rather than inform. Meaningful discourse must necessarily include a multitude of perspectives. In a polarized society, this hierarchal ordering of perspectives has a chilling effect on the production and expression of dissenting views.

Dissent, however, is both a critical component of a free and democratic society, and a crucial component in the development of critical thinking skills. It prevents a tyranny of the majority and prevents the relegation of unpopular thoughts to only the margins. Without dissent, our discourse would be limited and myopic. The ability to challenge convention and consider alternative perspectives is essential to knowledge acquisition and transfer.

Where polarization manifests and builds a home, the zero-sum approach to discourse and social cohesion naturally follows. Rather than seek common ground and understanding, we strive to win the argument by any means necessary. In such an environment it is easy to disregard those we disagree with as dullards and vilify their motives as inherently evil and misguided. It sends the everyday internet social justice warrior down endless rabbit holes looking for data and information to negate their "opponent's" arguments and "educate" them on the right facts.

What is consistent, however, in all these polarized arguments, both on the internet and in person, is that no one ever seems to convince anyone else to change their position. Equally troubling is that no one ever walks away having changed their own position.

I argue that the mere existence and availability of information does not automatically make us more informed, nor better suited to cooperate with others. I suggest that polarization of thought is enabled by technological systems that personalize, and simultaneously limit, the flow of objective information. Finally, I posit that dissent is critically important to gaining a more informed perspective of the world.

We all love our technology, our curated and personalized content, and the algorithmic suggestions we receive that make shopping or picking a restaurant so easy. What we love even more, however, is that most of the apps on our devices are free to use. You have to pay for access to the New York Times and the Wall Street Journal. You have to pay to read The Globe & Mail and the National Post., but Facebook, Instagram, and Google are all free. Then again, that too was explained by Tristan Harris, a former Google design ethicist, who stated:

"If you're not paying for the product, you are the product."

All that remains now is the question: how will you mobilize this information?

What if the Invisible Hand Guided Remote Work

Published by Seeking Veritas on Substack: Jan 23, 2024

Whether you love it or hate it, remote work is probably here to stay; but when did it get here? For many people, the 2020 global COVID pandemic was their first introduction to the concept of remote work. But is it new? Does it work? And are we missing an important employer option that could turn this entire conversation on its head?

Lockdowns during the COVID pandemic began with uncertainty. People spent the first couple of weeks wondering where to get toilet paper. Within a couple of months, everyone became experts in global supply chain management, offering their personal analysis about the pitfalls of just-in-time delivery. About the five-month mark, people experienced collective amnesia about the downsides of big family gatherings, thus was born family Zoom calls and virtual movie parties, much to the chagrin of those young folks who actually preferred the "and chill" part of "Netflix and chill"!

Meanwhile in corporate Zoom boardrooms, organizations were trying to figure out business continuity strategies, budget forecasts and whether it was time to start off-loading their capital assets. It's as if the world neatly divided itself into separate camps with no common playbook. In an abstract theoretical sense, this has little consequence; academics and activists are free to critique capitalism and profit orientation. In reality, there are interdependencies and sustainability considerations that must be considered in order to keep systems viable and operational.

We live in the age of information. We have access to more data in a few seconds than previous generations had in a lifetime, yet we seem to constantly under utilize this gift. For instance, this remote work conversation is hardly new. Like most things, we just renamed it, pretended it was novel, and acted as if we were trail blazers who reconfigured the future of work.

Remote or hybrid work has always been with us in some capacity. In previous iterations, remote work has gone by other names. In 1972, Jack Nilles told people he was engaged in "telecommuting" while explaining how he was working remotely on a complex NASA job and just like that, the phrase was coined. A famous article from 1979 in the Washington Post titled "Working From Home Can Save Gasoline" by Frank Schiff, an economist, is often credited with beginning to popularize the idea of working from home and led to the first conference about the subject, which took place in 1980.

In his article, Schiff was exploring ways to conserve gasoline consumption by suggesting a few workers could work from home one or two days a week. He cited advances in computerization and electronic chip-technology that he believed would change the nature of machinery. He forecasted that the new portable machines being used to record dictation, previously taken down in shorthand by secretaries in an office, would allow persons working at home to use the telephone to dictate directly into machines located in their offices. He even envisioned a "paperless office" given 20,000 pages could be reduced to very small proportions encoded on four-by-six-inch microfiche film sheets. By 1994, there was even a dedicated day in September called Employee Telecommuting Day.

In the early 2000s, the use of text-based pagers and Blackberry smart phones made working on the go much easier. People argued that the new technology would reduce inefficiency, improve communication, and reduce the need for centralized office space. All that excess time gained was meant to result in more leisure time, perhaps a four-day work week, and higher quality of social life. Well, we all know how that turned out.

To play devil's advocate, many arguments made in favour of telecommuting, remote, or hybrid scheduling, whatever you want to call it, have merit. There is a good case for environmental impact made by reduced travel. Project based work with clear outputs and limited collaboration are ideal for remote scheduling, assuming accountability is maintained. Some argue that eradicating all the unnecessary waste of time that occurs around the proverbial water cooler is a net gain for productivity; let's go ahead and concede that point too, even though the counter argument will probably be that there are an equal or greater number of distractions at home, arguably ones you care about more. But nonetheless, in theory, the point is coherent.

Advocates of remote work often argue that supervision is inherently demeaning and a holdover from previous patriarchal and classist systems. People should have greater autonomy over their work lives, they would argue. Many posit that remote work has benefits for mental wellbeing and therefore can be positively correlated with reduced turnover and lower rates of burnout. All these proposed benefits are used to demonstrate that remote work increases productivity and therefore should stay, even though the pandemic has ended.

For the sake of argument, let's concede all the points above and stipulate that there are several other benefits produced by remote work that I did not cover earlier. By conceding this position, I suppose I would have to support all those who state that people can be just as, or even more productive when working from home. Employers could concede those points for many positions within their organizations. They may argue that some client-facing positions require a limited presence on the job site, but preventing non-client-facing employees from working remotely would seem unreasonable by the logic presented by advocates of remote work. Although, I suppose that leaves employers with an interesting dilemma.

If people can work remotely and be just as efficient, why do they have to reside locally? Accepting that remote work increases productivity means employees can do the job from anywhere, assuming access to the required technology. If employers took a more global perspective, then standard wage considerations could be interpreted differently. Wages rates have historically been tied to the market value for labour. Other factors for consideration when calculating a fair wage would include the price of housing within a commutable distance, the consumer price index that influences cost of living, and the availability of skilled labour within a reasonable geographical distance. Labour costs generally make up a significant portion of operating expense, followed by capital assets (physical office spaces) and other operational overheads.

Employers could hire fully remote staff from places in the world where wage rates are more competitive. Since most lower wage earners live in the global south, the initiative to hire from these markets could also have a net benefit for global poverty and rates of employment. For significantly less money than the remote worker who lives down the street, organizations could hire more people while still realizing reductions in operating costs. One could argue that global equity demands that we stop privileging domestic remote labour while simultaneously devaluing the global workforce. In a global economy where labour can travel virtually anywhere and capital can pursue the best return on their investment, corporations could let the laws of demand and supply be the invisible hand.

If people don't need to come to the office, they probably don't need to live down the street. Is it time to globally democratize employment or should people return to work?

Transferable Leadership Skills to Navigate VUCA

Published by Seeking Veritas on Substack: Nov 21, 2023

"When you make decisions alone, you gratify your ego, but you're relying on partial information. Ignorant like Icarus, you fly too close to the sun. Leaders need a new approach that engages everyone to solve problems."
– Garcia and Fischer, 2023

A lot has changed over my nearly two decades as a post-secondary educator, and almost three decades in the Canadian workforce. The ways of doing business have been drastically changed; new technologies have altered not just processes but also norms. It is easy to forget that if we measured Google, social media, smartphones and the internet-of-things in human chronology, they are all still in the bratty teenage years. The OEBM (Old Economic Business Model) has gone the way of the telegram or dial-up internet, and our new precarious gig economy is characterized by volatility, uncertainty, complexity, and ambiguity (VUCA), yet some things have remained fairly consistent.

Leadership skills are transferable skills that have potential benefits to many different areas of life. Here are five leadership principles that I believe have had a net positive impact in my life and career. They are lessons I often conveyed when I taught leadership and management courses.

Consistency in Application

Humans are pattern dependent in many ways; a fair argument can even be made for the predictability of human thought and action. History provides significant evidence of our inability to learn from our past. Developing the capacity to detect recurring patterns early and often allow us to read situational cues more accurately and efficiently. Leaders benefit from consistency because people are more likely to trust those who offer a degree of predictability. When people enter interactions with a high degree of uncertainty, trust is hard to establish, and rapport is even harder to develop. Having consistency in application creates confidence in those around you, as it establishes the norms and the expectations that surround interactions.

Clarity in Communication
Clarity is a central feature to effective communications because no where is the law of parsimony more crucial than in the transmission of an idea. If you want people to understand you, clarity will take you further than rhetoric. Organizations serve a distinct purpose, pretending otherwise only creates scope creep. When leaders communicate with clarity, people in the organization can make informed choices about participation and commitment.

However, communication is complex; we are always communicating even when we don't realize it. Any time the verbal and nonverbal communication are incongruous, people will always read more into the nonverbal. By some accounts, it is argued that 55% of communication is body language, about 38% is tonality and cadence, and only 7% of all communication is dependent on the actual words. So, while it is undoubtedly important to watch our words, it is equally important to ensure clarity in our messaging.

Authenticity in Character
Ask five people what kind of leader you should be, and you will get at least eight different answers. Trendy leadership theories are constantly emerging, many have merit, some have new packaging, but here is a simple approach: Be your authentic self because everyone else is taken. Having a few stable principles to guide your decision-making is far better than having many convoluted ones. Say what you mean and do what you say. That level of authenticity is easier to develop when you pay close attention to the first two points: Consistency in application and clarity in communication.

Diligence in Managing Risk
A savvy leader knows that alienating the people who disagree out the gate is the surest way to ensure you don't get far. There will always be a segment who support you and a segment that oppose you. It's the third group, the undecided, where you need to focus your energy. Organizations are run by people and people are susceptible to trends and blind spots. The effective management of risks both near and far is what creates a sustainable organization that can withstand the tumult of rapid social and technological change. In our highly connected world, seemingly unconnected events on the

other side of the planet can influence and even disrupt business operations. Effective management of risk is even more critical as the world shrinks. While we may never be able to plan for every possible scenario, the old risk management objectives still have value, namely, reduce the ratio of unfavourable events to total events. Where possible, mitigate, avoid, or transfer and when unavoidable, figure out your risk tolerance and operate within it.

Be Driven by Purpose
Lead with purpose, not with rigid rules. Adaptive and efficient organizations need to be responsive. This necessitates clearly identifying the choke points within the organizational structure that slows decision-making. Highly effective organizations decentralize decision-making, because the top-down command and control model rarely works quickly enough to keep pace with rapidly developing situations. The loss of traditional control can be unnerving, even uncomfortable, but it doesn't have to be. We have a natural tendency to think in extremes; giving up some control does not imply a free for all. Organizations still need to coalesce around simple foundational principles that serve as guardrails for informed decision-making at every level of the organization.

For me, developing the ability to be consistent, clear, judicious, authentic, and purposeful has served me well in life. In the spirit of making knowledge accessible and democratizing information, I share this with you, take an idea, maybe leave one in the comments too. That after all is how community building is done.

Finding Stupidity Down a Rabbit Hole

Published by Seeking Veritas on Substack: Sep 14, 2023

During one my many sleepless nights, I found a rabbit hole and decided to jump down it. I binge read several short stories that night, hoping my eyes would tire and sleep would come. Unfortunately for me, once I embark down a rabbit hole, I can often spend the entire night reading and inadvertently miss the part where I was supposed to sleep. But it is on these late-night thought excursions, fuelled by curiosity, that I come across works I may not have otherwise read. That's how I encountered Carlo M. Cipolla and his Basic Laws of Stupidity. The takeaways from that story have stuck with me for decades,

In 1976, Cipolla, a professor of economic history at UC Berkeley, published an essay outlining the fundamental laws of a force he perceived as humanity's greatest existential threat, namely Stupidity.

These are Cipolla's five fundamental laws of stupidity:

LAW 1 – Always and inevitably, everyone underestimates the number of stupid individuals in circulation.
Cipolla argued that we all know stupid people exist, but we underestimate both the number of them and their impact on society. Perhaps it's our nature or maybe our socialization that prompts us to look at others in the most charitable light, even when the evidence does not support it. After all stupidity, or whatever kinder name you wish to call it by, is a regular feature of the human condition. We all have experience dealing with someone we perceive that way, even if we don't vocalize it.

LAW 2 – The probability that a certain person (will) be stupid is independent of any other characteristic of that person.
What we do know from lived experience is that stupidity does not discriminate. The condition is fairly universal

and exists within every culture, gender, nationality, ethnicity, and political ideology. Cipolla often quoted his father, who often suggested that the best course was to assume half of everyone you meet is below average. This sounds like a fair hypothesis supported by basic arithmetic.

LAW 3 – A stupid person is a person who causes losses to another person or to a group of persons while himself deriving no gain and even possibly incurring losses.

For Cipolla, stupid people cause losses to others while deriving no benefits personally. He didn't consider them to be ill-willed, but rather merely incapable of seeing the effects of their actions in a broader context. Not benefitting, or potentially losing out, in this case is not a virtue but an unintended consequence. The inability to see downstream impacts may be a by-product of our hyper focus on living in the here and now. While I'm all for being present, we need to be cognizant about the ripple effects of our decisions. It is arguably a critical condition for civic engagement and leadership.

LAW 4 – Non-stupid people always underestimate the damaging power of stupid individuals. In particular, non-stupid people constantly forget that at all times and places, and under any circumstances, to deal and/or

associate with stupid people always turns out to be a costly mistake.

His best advice to people who are not stupid is to avoid the stupid people whenever they are encountered. "Stupid people are deadly dangerous because reasonable people find it difficult to imagine and understand stupid behavior." It is the state of disbelief or the inability to comprehend stupidity that exposes the rest of the population to the misfortunes of dealing with them.

I once watched a comedy skit featuring John Cleese on the subject of stupidity; his contribution to the subject is both entertaining and eerily accurate. Cleese quips that people who are stupid lack the precise skill needed to know that they are stupid, thereby leaving us all in the precarious situation of living with oblivious ignorance. A significant social disadvantage for everyone involved.

LAW 5 – A stupid person is the most dangerous type of person. (Corollary: a stupid person is more dangerous than a corrupt person.)
He argued that stupid people act in unpredictable ways. That lack of predictability makes stupid people incredibly dangerous because their motivation is not easily discernible, even to themselves. I draw upon Socrates here, who posited that the greatest good is knowledge and the greatest evil, ignorance. But he also

emphasized that the real problem lies with "Double Ignorance." Socrates defined double ignorance as not being aware of one's ignorance while thinking that one knows!

As I lay reflecting on this article and sleep finally seemed to plausibly be on the horizon, another rabbit hole appeared! I wonder what David Dunning and Justin Kruger would say if they sat down with Carlo Cipolla's favourite group... Alas, that might be a wonderland for another night. Then again, do I really need sleep? Stay tuned...

Section 3 -
FINDING OUR COMMON HUMANITY AMIDST CONFLICT AND DIVISION

Summary

In an age defined by rapid change and growing complexity, humanity faces profound challenges. From geopolitical tensions to cultural clashes, and from ideological divides to interpersonal misunderstandings, the fractures in our world often seem insurmountable. Yet, amid this turmoil lies an undeniable truth: our shared humanity is the thread that binds us.

How can we reconcile our differences while honoring the dignity and uniqueness of every individual? Central and pertinent to this question is the concept of Diversity, Equity, and Inclusion (DEI). These principles have gained prominence as tools to address historical injustices and build a more inclusive society. However, their implementation—often associated with what critics and proponents alike call the "woke agenda"—has sparked both passionate support and fervent resistance. Some view DEI initiatives as essential for creating fairness and belonging, while others perceive them as divisive or overly prescriptive.

These articles do not shy away from the complexities and controversies of these debates. Instead, they aim to engage with them thoughtfully, recognizing that progress often requires navigating discomfort.

More importantly, this journey is about rediscovering the humanity that transcends our labels and affiliations. What unites us as people? How can we learn to listen, empathize, and collaborate across our differences? These are not merely philosophical questions but urgent, practical imperatives in a world that needs healing.

Whether you're an advocate for systemic change, a skeptic of current trends, or simply someone searching for hope in divisive times, you are invited to explore the nuances and uncover the potential for common ground. Because at the end of the day, it is not our ideologies or agendas that define us—it is our capacity to care for one another.

Unwelcome & Unwanted: The South Asian Struggle in Contemporary Canada

Published by Seeking Veritas on Substack: Sept 1, 2024

Hate and slurs against South Asians have increased significantly since January 2023 and it feels like a resurgence of the 90s era intolerance

The 2020 World Values Survey places Canada amongst the most racially tolerant countries in the world, with less than five per cent of those surveyed saying that they would not want to have "people of another race" as their neighbours, unfortunately for immigrants exposed to the less tolerant in Canadian society that survey brings very little comfort.

A hate crime reported to police in Peterborough, Ontario on July 26, 2024, brought to light the experience of a man of Sikh ancestry who was spat on and had his turban knocked off and stepped on, another in a long list of growing incidents with troubling implications for the Indian diaspora in Canada. According to Statistics Canada, hate crimes toward South Asian communities, a demographic covering India, Pakistan, Bangladesh, Nepal, and Sri Lanka increased by 143% between 2019 to 2022, a trend that seems to be continuing across the province of Ontario.

Beyond physical acts of intolerance and hate, the online world has been relentless in its vitriolic disdain for South Asians. From fringe platforms to mainstream social media there appears to be no refuge from the ire of a vocal minority of hateful Canadians calling South Asians "Pakis" (a derogatory term originating in the United Kingdom) and "Pajeets" (a derogatory made-up Indian name originating on 4chan in 2015) while expressing their disdain for "brown people" in the community and "their" neighbourhoods.

The Global Project Against Hate and Racism reported a large increase in hate and slurs directed toward South Asians globally since January 2023. *"Anxieties around losing jobs, the perceived 'subversion' of white people, and both distrust and anger towards South Asians who are blamed for these problems are prevalent across platforms... The phrase, 'they have to go back,' which advocates for the deportation of Indian immigrants en masse from Canada, is worryingly reminiscent of a trend gaining popularity in Europe called "remigration," which argues for ethnically cleansing the continent of non-Europeans through forced deportations"* the report states. A prominent far-right influencer, Canadian military veteran Jeremy Mackenzie of the white supremacist movement Diagolon routinely advocates hate against South Asians and calls for first world countries to quarantine India otherwise Indians will colonize every first world country as part of a "Great Replacement" of white people.

Since January 2023, slurs directed at South Asians on fringe platforms such as 4chan, Telegram, and Truth Social have been rising exponentially, blaming the community for "replacing" white people. On platforms such as Facebook, hate directed at South Asians has become a common occurrence. On Instagram racism directed at South Asians routinely fill the comment sections. A partnered study, undertaken in early 2023 between the Angus Reid Institute (ARI) and the CRRF

(Canadian Race Relations Foundation), allowed for a comparison between groups of Asian Canadians. At least one-quarter of all South Asians sampled reported that they faced discrimination or harassment over the past year.

In a CBC article Nandini Tirumala, Program Director for the Windsor Essex Anti-Hate Youth Collective, at the South Asian Centre of Windsor, commented that for international students dealing with learning a new culture, being away from family and coping with financial pressures, also having to focus on racism can be debilitating. *"I think a lot of this is propelled by the economic conditions that have started to happen in the country. When people see there are no jobs, there's inflation, we're not able to find affordable housing, they want to find someone to blame. And oftentimes, it's the immigrants who are blamed."*

A Sad 90s Re-run
When I delivered my TEDx Talk in 2022 I shared my experiences from the 1990s as a new immigrant with a South Asian background. The Ontario I found myself in had recently seen a large influx of new immigrants from South East Asia. According to Statistics Canada while the majority of 1980s entrants were European or North American, most of those arriving in mid-nineties were Asian. Interestingly the Asian cohort of the nineties had

higher levels of education and were more likely to speak an official language than earlier European cohorts.

"About 2.2 million immigrants came to Canada in the 1990s, accounting for over half the population growth during that period, and representing the largest number of entrants for any decade in the past century. Nearly half (46%) of those who arrived in the 1990s (1.0 million people) were aged 25 to 44...This group contributed much to the growth of Canada's labour force during the decade."

The 1990s was also the first time I encountered the term, 'Paki', which I initially did not realize was intended to be derogatory. I remember clarifying for people early on that I was in fact Indian not Pakistani. Nobody back then seemed to care much for my clarification, to many it was a distinction without a difference. In Canada, I was a stranger and a visible minority, another term that I was previously unfamiliar with but one that would soon become a defining feature of my new identity. The term 'Paki' as I experienced it was not intended to signify a country of origin but rather the state of being different and unwanted.

I often heard harsh exhalations like "Go back to where you came from; get back on the boat; you people come here and take our jobs; and you people are a drain on our country". I struggled with those words, they cut deeply and often made me second guess if this was truly a better place to be. The reality was the Canadian landscape was changing, the shades around them were darkening, the culture was shifting and that made people feel uncomfortable. For many of us immigrants however being tethered to stereotypes of our country of origin can be a barrier to full inclusion and a prime mover in the decision to socially and culturally isolate.

It has been almost thirty years since I arrived in Canada. For a long time now, I believed the situation was improving. Perhaps I have assimilated more thoroughly, or perhaps the sting of being rebuked early on has become less emotionally charged over time. Today the labels imposed upon me by those less welcoming have less of a psychological impact as I have grown into my own Canadian identity. Witnessing recent racial and cultural hate faced by new immigrants is disheartening, it opens old wounds, and it pains me to see newcomers facing the same obstacles I had to face in the 90s. Their current struggles were my past struggles, their situation reminds me of the importance of empathy because I've been where they are, and I know it doesn't feel good.

Between 2016 and 2021, Canada brought in approximately 1.3 million immigrants. Census data from 2021 shows that migrants from India, the Philippines and China were the three most numerous groups of recent immigrants arriving in Canada. Around 18.6% of recent immigrants were born in India, 11.4% in the Philippines and 8.9% in China. It would appear that the visible presence of these minority groups has created a resurgence in the 90s era hate filled pushback. I feel their pain, it is disheartening to come to a country known for its friendly tolerant people, with hopes and dreams of making a better life for your children, only to be made to feel unwanted and unwelcome. Worse still to be labelled a pariah!

If only more people knew that Canada's immigration policies have rarely prioritized humanitarianism; our immigration policy is firmly rooted in economic development and growth of the Canadian economy. Immigrants serve to fill labour gap shortages, maximize investment capital, and increase the tax base that is consistently shrinking due to our aging population. If facts could counter bigotry I would offer the following:

- More than 80% of the immigrants admitted in recent years are under 45 years old, meaning they will have plenty of working years in Canada. - That means more taxes and more spending in the economy.
- The income tax paid by working Canadians pays for health care, education and other vital services. In 1980, there were roughly 6 workers for every retiree. In 2015, there were 4 workers for every retiree. By

2030, when 5 million Canadians are set to retire, the ratio will be down to only 3 workers for every retiree.
- Without immigrants to help offset the trends of an aging population, Canada would not be able to offer the same level of services to its residents into the future.
- Immigrants account for 32% of all business owners with paid staff. They create local jobs in numerous sectors of the economy.
- International students contribute more than $21 billion to the economy every year through student spending and tuition. Their spending amounts to more than Canada's exports of auto parts, lumber or aircraft.

Hate the sin, pity the sinner

Published by Seeking Veritas on Substack: Oct 29, 2024

The antidote to hate cannot be more hate; the response to repugnant speech should be considered speech. In the face of hatred this article calls for humanity

On Saturday October 19th, 2024, the burned deceased body of Gursimran Kaur, a 19-year-old young woman was found in a Nova Scotia Walmart bakery oven. She was originally from India and had immigrated to Canada with her mother about two years before. Halifax Regional Police have said a criminal investigation is currently ongoing and for this reason I won't speculate on the specifics of the incident as there is a great deal that is unknown at this time.

The focus of this article is not on the actual event, but rather the social media reaction to the tragic death of this young woman. A couple of months ago I wrote an article titled Unwelcome and Unwanted, it focused on the concerning trends related to hate directed at South Asians in Canada. I really wish I wasn't writing another piece on the same subject so soon.

In that article I shared a story from July 26, 2024, about a man of Sikh ancestry who was spat on and had his turban knocked off and stepped on in Peterborough, Ontario. According to Statistics Canada, hate crimes toward☐South Asian communities, has increased recently by 143%, evidence of troubling implications for the Indian diaspora in Canada. - And here we are again.

Social Media Cancer
In the aftermath of the tragic death of Gursimran Kaur, the social media trolls were quick to spread hateful and derogatory commentary about the incident. The posts below provide a sample of the vitriolic hate that is currently circulating.

- *Rest in Deodorant*

- *Just one?*
- *2 billion to go*
- *And just like that, that Walmart stank like curry for hours*
- *One down many to go...clean [sic] canada from [sic] endian infestation*
- *In's a [soc] indian guys it's ok guys they are an invasive species*

It is tempting to respond to these posts with righteous indignation, however the antidote to hate cannot be more hate. I wouldn't even demand that their abhorrent posts be taken down, de-platforming them should not be the logical choice in my opinion. I suggest that the response to repugnant speech should be considered speech. I do not make this suggestion lightly. Those messages undoubtedly spread hateful sentiments. The nature of algorithmic incentives will result in them going viral, that is inevitable and unavoidable. What we should do is respond by summoning the better angels of our humanity.

It is important to recognize that 80% of the viral content on these social media sites are generated by approximately 10% of users. The implication of this skewed content creation distribution is that it falsely creates a sense of consensus. But their views are NOT the consensus, these sentiments do NOT represent the best of our Canadian values. I have heard people say these are conservative white people who hate immigrants, I disagree with that characterization as well. These sentiments do NOT represent all white people, and they are NOT representative of conservatives writ large; at best it is a crude caricature of conservatism.

Let's be clear, and let's say it repeatedly, these views represent a small fraction of people, albeit people with a large microphone attached to parasitic technologies. Their views have been fermented by hate, convoluted by fears, and influenced by economic and social change which threatens their identity. We should not look upon them with hate, we should feel sorry for them. I probably wouldn't call them a basket of deplorables, but they appear to lack the critical thinking skills necessary for functioning in a complex society - it must be very challenging to be that myopic.

I urge you no matter how difficult, to not hide these posts from others, don't delete them, rather talk to people you know about it, expose it for what it is, UN-CANADIAN, UN-DEMOCRATIC, and utterly INDECENT.

Social media has become an undeniable force in shaping the landscape of our culture. As of 2024, there are 5.17 billion people actively using social media globally. The average user engages with 6.7 different platforms and the average time spent per user per day is 2 hours 20 minutes. These platforms have quickly become the primary sources of news and information for many users. Is it any wonder why hateful lies spread around the world so feverishly before the truth even wakes up in the morning?!

An olive branch and a devil's bargain
If you are indifferent to the posts above, if you support the posts, or plan to pile on even in private, then I offer this.

If you believe that there is a justifiable debate to be had about Canadian immigration policy, many South Asians agree too. If you believe that housing prices and inflation cause economic stress, many South Asians agree too. If you believe unemployment rates cause frustration and anger, many South Asians agree too. If you believe that wokeism and calls for segregated spaces solely for coloured people is vacuous and misguided, many South Asians agree too.

So, here's the devil's bargain - If you want to inundate us with a cacophony of putrid verbal dehumanizing rhetoric, my generation and the ones that came before us are no strangers to such antagonism. From the Portuguese to the British, from Komagata Maru to Idi Amin we have seen it all, so ... bring it! - Just leave our kids out of it!

The victim of this tragic event in Nova Scotia was a 19-year-old girl, a child, someone's daughter, someone's sister, someone's family, someone's loved one - What if it was your child, your daughter, your sister, your family, your loved one? What common decency would you demand? What humanity would you hope for?

Unsung Heroes

Published by Seeking Veritas on Substack: Jun 8, 2023

How much black history do you actually remember? Do you think or even talk about it between March and January each year? With February 2023 now behind us, we must wait another year before the next iteration of Black History Month. The annual government-designated month-long observance not only reminds us of how easy it is to pay lip service to the remembrance of the people of the African diaspora; it also reminds us that, in our collective mind, not all heroes are created equal. That many stories are forgotten for the benefit of grand narratives. That many unsung heroes are hidden behind the veil of the most popular stories. In Canadian schools we cover a great deal of American content; we played all the American greatest hits — the Kings, the Parks, and the Obamas. Perhaps some secondary schools dug deeper and gave honourable mentions to Booker T. Washington, Dubois, and Douglass, but who knows?

It is an unfortunate Canadian fact that we forget our own heroes as we give the stage to our neighbours. Think Mary Ann Shadd Cary (1823-1893), the first black woman to publish a newspaper in North America. She also established a racially integrated school in Windsor, Ontario. Remember her? What of Lincoln Alexander (1922-2012), the first black Member of Parliament? In 1985, he was appointed as Canada's Lieutenant Governor and became the first visible minority to hold this position. Remember him? And what about Violet King (1929-1982), the first black woman lawyer in Canada? The list could go on, but I'll keep it brief. Other than Viola Davis, whose face is now on the 10-dollar bill, how many of those names do you actually remember? Or even recognize?

Play with me for a moment and read the following passage I have dramatically recreated for you. Identify the person I am referring to (without reading ahead) and try to remember the first time you heard the story.

You've definitely heard this story before, as it is a commonly told American civil rights story. Come with me on this journey back through a prominent black history month story retold every year.

It's March 2, 1955, the cooler months are ending, and the temperature rises steadily. Every day now we anticipate the heat, which only worsens as months go by here in the South. Today, my school, the Booker T. Washington School has let out, and the streets are getting busier. I stare down the road and consider my walk home. I look over my shoulder and the green and gold bus appears. Friends are waiting, and I think I will join them. We board the bus, which is almost full, and the four of us shuffle down the aisle five, maybe six rows from the front. This is where we have to sit, that line, always that line, invisible yet clearly demarcated by our reality.

As the bus is about to leave, one last woman gets on, but there isn't a seat available. She slowly walks down the aisle, past three rows then four, eyes narrowed, her pale white sullen face expressionless almost. She walks all the way to the line, that invisible line, and there is no need to go further. What is beyond the line is of no importance to her. She turns back towards the driver, her options are in that direction, not the other. There is no need to look further.

I see the driver's eyes in his rear-view mirror. The woman and he exchange glances, and he blinks slowly. I can't hear the sound of the road anymore, nor can I feel the breeze through the window. That confined space feels smaller now, the contraction of space is familiar, almost like that part of a breath we are used to taking constantly yet somehow always feels tighter during the inhale. "I need those seats," the driver's voice bellowed from the front. That was it, just four words, the same four words, heard countless times by countless people before. Nothing to process, the action and the reaction had been normalized, routinized; the script had been written a long time ago. You are supposed to follow the script; it is the normal order.

The two people sitting across the aisle and the one sitting beside me immediately rise from their seats. They walk further back and remain standing as the script dictates. My feet feel heavy, weighing me down like they are stuck to the floor of the bus. I don't say a word, I don't have a word to say, there is no word in the script. In my periphery, I can see the empty seats across the aisle from me, they are available, they are perfectly good seats. Those seats were vacated by two people so as to benefit the one person standing. Not an elderly person. Not someone who needed two seats. Just one person who walked up to the line, saw no room and expected the line to be moved.

Yes, that invisible line demarcated by our reality; it shifted while I sat in my seat. Now I was on the wrong side, and I haven't even moved. I hear rumbling voices, angry and confused, I cannot make out what they are saying, it is all happening so fast and yet somehow everything feels like it is moving in slow motion. My feet feel like they are in thick mud, the muscles in my legs are tense, my back is stiff, and I am acutely aware of the bead of sweat rolling down from my hair line. Those open seats across from me are not yet good enough, they are not yet usable, because the line shifted below me while I sat in the same place, and I am now in the wrong row. Under the twisted understanding and application of the Plessey doctrine, this is not separate because she would have to share the row with me if she sat down. That could not happen, she had to be closer to the front and I had to be behind the line.
A voice tells me to get up. I cannot tell if it's coming from behind me, from in front of me, or from within me. My body isn't moving. It feels as though Harriet Tubman's hands are pushing me down on one

shoulder and Sojourner Truth's hands are pushing down on the other. I paid my fare, I should have rights, and she can sit on one of the available seats. I stay behind the line and the line moves. The bus doesn't stop, but the air gets heavier. The space seems smaller; that confined space is closing in. Then the bus jerks and comes to a stop. The silence is deafening, although I am not entirely certain it is really silent on that bus. The driver is having an animated conversation with two policemen at the junction at which the bus had come to a stop.

Within a few minutes, which seems like an hour to me, the two policemen board the bus. The sound of their boots as they walk past the first few rows of the bus sounds like an army marching towards me; it is all consuming as I stare down at the floor, afraid but defiant. I paid my fare; I should have rights. That is all I could focus on. How is this separate but equal. I do not feel equal, I am not equal, not in this moment or any other moment before this.

A commotion followed, I do not fully remember the conversation, although conversation is hardly a fair description of what transpired. My books went flying and I felt a strong hand grab my arm, I don't know how I ended up off the bus, I was told later that it was an uncouth display as I was kicked and dragged backwards off the bus, the details of which are buried and recessed deep in my pained subconscious. I was in the back of the police car, and I remember clearly when they asked me to stick my hands out the window. I felt the cold hard steel push against my wrist, my bones felt every vibration as the single strand of the handcuff pushed against my arm, the loud sound of the ratchets clicking as the handcuffs tightened.

After her arrest, the community rallied, and a number of black leaders raised money for her defence. At the time, local black leaders believed that her case was an appropriate one to litigate all the way to the United States Supreme Court, as part of a broader effort to overturn segregation laws in the South. A little-known, twenty-six-year-old preacher of the Dexter Avenue Baptist Church made his political debut fighting her arrest. On December 5, 1955, forty thousand African American bus passengers boycotted the Montgomery Alabama bus system. Black leaders met to form the Montgomery Improvement Association (MIA), electing the young pastor as their president. On May 11, 1956, she testified in a Montgomery federal court hearing about her actions on the bus. Because the case challenged the constitutionality of a state statute, the case was brought before a three-judge U.S. District

Court panel. On June 19, 1956, the panel ruled two-to-one that segregation on Alabama's intrastate buses was unconstitutional, that Montgomery's segregation codes "deny and deprive plaintiffs and other Negro citizens similarly situated of the equal protection of the laws and due process of law secured by the Fourteenth Amendment."

On December 17, 1956, the Supreme Court rejected city and state appeals to reconsider their decision. Three days later, on the December 20, 1956, the U.S. Supreme Court ruled that segregation on the buses must end and affirmed the June ruling. That same day, the young preacher and the MIA voted to end the three-hundred-and-eighty-one-day bus boycott. The Montgomery buses were integrated the following day. The pastor, in an address at a mass meeting at Holt Street Baptist Church, stated that "separate facilities are inherently unequal, and that the old Plessy Doctrine of separate but equal is no longer valid, either sociologically or legally." That then-defiant act was one of the most significant moments, even a watershed event in the American civil rights movement. Most of us can name the courageous woman who refused to yield her seat and the young preacher that led the way.

The passage above is a story I use in a diversity lecture I have delivered both for students on campus and in presentations for corporate clients. At the end of the story, I always ask the audience if they are familiar with it. The answers are always an emphatic, "Yes of course!" I follow with, "Who is the pastor?" Almost all of them in unison shout, "The Reverend Martin Luther King Jr!" And finally, I ask, "Who is the woman?" And the response is just as quick and confident, "Rosa Parks!" I usually pause until the room has settled into a quiet silence, a practice that I think is unsettling to the vast majority of my students and people in the general public who come to hear me speak. As I stand at the front of the room, I see people begin to shift and squirm in their seats.

At this point, they have a quizzical look on their face; some of them checking their schedules wondering if they are, in fact, in the wrong room. Perhaps this is a civics class, not the course they were enrolled in or the presentation they had signed up for. Others wonder if something happened somewhere else in the room that has forced me to stop; there are always at least a couple of people who figure that the eccentric professor at the front of the room has forgotten his next line. What none of them seem to do, however, is wonder if there is something wrong with the responses they provided.

Why would they? They have heard this story many times before-from elementary to high school to post-secondary. In history classes and in civic classes. From social studies to black history month. It's a defining story of the American Civil Rights movement. A story they can't not know. Many remember watching the news when then-U.S. President Barrack Obama unveiled the Rosa Park statue on February 27, 2013. The New York Times wrote, "the statue of Rosa Parks captured her waiting to be arrested in 1955, after she refused to give up her seat for a white passenger on a crowded segregated bus in Montgomery, Alabama. She is seated, clutching her purse as she looks out of an unseen window waiting for the police."

After what I'm sure seems like an eternity to the audience, I begin my lecture again. I tell them they were half correct and, fortunately for them, this was not a graded activity because they would have all received a whopping fifty percent. Not quite an F, but a far cry from an A. The pastor is none other than the Reverend Dr. Martin Luther King Jr, but the woman in the story is not Rosa Parks. I remind them of the very first line of the story I narrated, "It is March 2, 1955..." That would be a full nine months before the arrest of Rosa Parks on December 1, 1955.

As a point of fact, I could have told them a story about
Aurelia Browder, a thirty-six-year-old woman who was
arrested in April of 1955, or of Mary Louise Smith an
eighteen-year-old woman arrested in October of 1955, or
of Susie McDonald commonly known as Miss Sue, a
woman in her seventies who was also arrested in October
1955. Instead, I told them the story from March 2, 1955,
about a fifteen-year-old girl named Claudette Colvin, the
first person to be arrested for challenging Montgomery's
bus segregation policies. What all those women have in
common is that they were all arrested for refusing to give
up their seats on a Montgomery, Alabama bus before
Rosa Parks.

It was these four women who we must call by name,
Aurelia Browder, Susie McDonald, Claudette Colvin, and
Mary Louise Smith, who served as plaintiffs in the legal
action challenging Montgomery's segregated public
transportation system. It was their case known as
Browder v. Gayle that the district court, and ultimately
the U.S. Supreme Court, would use to strike down
segregation on buses. So, why did no one in those
audiences respond with Colvin's name? It is not merely a
matter of forgetting a lesson from primary or secondary
school. Narratives are shaped by history, the contexts of
their time, and the inevitable myth and ideology building
that occurs over time. The reality is the lessons about

Colvin and the other plaintiffs in the Browder v Gayle case are not generally taught.

You can draw a direct line from the decision-making and strategy from 1955 to our modern era. At that time, prominent members of her own community felt Colvin's social station was not ideal for the launch of a social movement. Her father mowed lawns, and her mother was a maid. They lived in King Hill, a very poor section of Montgomery. She was a teenager considered "too young and too dark-skinned to be an effective symbol of injustice for the rest of the nation." When Claudette Colvin and her family members were asked about the incident more than forty years later, they would explain that her family never discussed the event much. Claudette's mother believed they shouldn't say anything that took away from Rosa Parks, who was already considered the mother of the civil rights movement.

Claudette's position was fairly straightforward. She said, "Let the people know Rosa Parks was the right person for the boycott. But also let them know that the attorneys took four other women to the Supreme Court to challenge the law that led to the end of segregation." Colvin's mother's position demonstrates the lived understanding of people whose social position is routinely challenged, whose sense of identity is questioned. She pragmatically stated to her own daughter, "Let Rosa be the one. White people aren't going to bother Rosa — her skin is lighter than yours and they like her."

Rosa Parks was neither handcuffed nor jailed, and she was released after being found guilty of disorderly conduct. She also had to pay a ten-dollar fine plus four dollars in court costs. Parks was convicted under city law, and her lawyer filed a notice of appeal. While her appeal was tied up in the State Court of Appeals, the Browder v. Gayle case ruling was settled. In November 1957, in a general settlement of the bus boycott cases, Martin Luther King Jr. and Rosa Parks dropped their appeals to the state Supreme Court and paid their fines. Rosa Parks, who died in 2005, received the highest civilian honours from the American White House and Congress. Claudette Colvin, on the other hand, has a street named after her. She also has her name on a granite marker along with the other plaintiffs in the Browder v Gayle case, the marker is placed near a life-sized statue of Rosa Parks in Montgomery, Alabama that was unveiled in 2019 by Mayor Steven Reed, the first African American mayor of Montgomery.

My intent has always been to get my audience to explore the benefits of being open-minded and willing to explore a variety of perspectives. Why? To grow our collective reservoir of available objective knowledge. Yet each time

I discover that making people uncomfortable often is the leading cause of mental shutdown. Even though I utilize the same speech with audiences at different age and life stages, the consistency in reaction between college age students and the general public perplexes me. There seems to be a greater commonality and fondness for the myths and ideologies that shape our worldviews, sometimes with little regard for historical nuance.

Martin Luther King's Pulitzer Prize-winning biographer, David J. Garrow, famously said, "It's an important reminder that crucial change is often ignited by very plain, unremarkable people who then disappear." This article was written as a tribute to all those people our social icons are meant to represent. This one is for all the unsung heroes out there past, present and future.

Napalm the Destroyer: The Burning of Tokyo

Published by Seeking Veritas on Substack: Aug 1, 2023

"From January 1944 to August 1945, the U.S. dropped 157,000 tons of bombs on Japanese cities, according to the U.S. Strategic Bombing Survey. It estimated that 333,000 people were killed. Other estimates are significantly higher. Fifteen million of the 72 million Japanese people were left homeless." – Tampa Bay Times

I watched the movie Oppenheimer a few days ago. (No spoiler alerts required here; as a cinephile, I would never ruin a movie for someone else. So read on, I assure you I

do not give anything about the movie away.) There was a passing line in the film about the bombing of Tokyo that caught my attention; it is easy to miss if you are not familiar with the story. It inspired this post.

The movie, along with all the hype it is generating, is sure to spurn at least a few conversations about the atomic bomb, Hiroshima, and Nagasaki. Let me state unequivocally, those are important conversations. Hiroshima marked the first time a single weapon capable of such mass destruction was employed.

Little Boy and the Fat Man
On August 6, 1945, the bomb dropped on Hiroshima, nicknamed "Little Boy", killed approximately 70,000 people within minutes. It was followed three days later on August 9, 1945, by the bombing of Nagasaki that instantly took the lives of another 46,000 people. The Americans nicknamed the second bomb "Fat Man." Both bombs accounted for countless more lives lost in the aftermath.

The use of the atomic bomb arguably set in the motion the nuclear arms race and untold atrocities in the pursuit of greater more destructive weaponry. But neither of those days get the horrific record of being the bombing event that killed the most Japanese people in a single event. That had actually happened almost four months

previously, when the US Air Force killed 100,000
Japanese people, mostly civilians, in Tokyo.

Burning Cities and the People Who Live in Them
On March 10th, 1945, the US Airforce conducted an aerial
bombing mission they called Operation Meetinghouse.
They sent in more than 300 American B-29 bombers and
dropped 1,500 tons of firebombs on the Japanese capital
of Tokyo. An area with tightly packed wooden houses, it
was a target intentionally selected for its high
flammability and population density. As the Japanese
people slept, the American bombers approached under
the cover of darkness. Between 1:30 a.m. and 3:00 a.m.
the Americans unleashed 500,000 M-69 bombs: each one
clustered in groups of 38. The clusters would separate
during their descent and small parachutes would carry
each bomblet to the ground. The jellied gasoline (napalm)
inside the metal casings would ignite seconds after
hitting something solid and shoot the flaming gel onto
the surrounding surfaces. They burnt the city down that
night.

The American Major General Curtis LeMay was the
officer in charge of strategic bombing. He utilized U.S.
military research on the flammability of Japanese
buildings in developing the aggressive tactic of dropping
firebombs at night on population centres. The strategy
was simple, in that if they couldn't take out the factories,

they could kill the people who worked in them. As many as 100,000 Japanese people were killed and another million injured, most of them civilians. The bombs incinerated an area of approximately 16 square miles to ash. A million people were left homeless. The death toll that night exceeded that of the atomic bombings of Hiroshima and Nagasaki later that year.

Irony and Hypocrisy

There was a cruel irony at play. In 1939, US President Franklin Roosevelt had urged world leaders to not use "the inhuman barbarism of bombing civilian populations." By 1945 the American government weren't as concerned about that issue. The United States Strategic Bombing Survey later wrote that *"probably more persons lost their lives by fire at Tokyo in a six-hour period than at any time in the history of man."*

Eyewitnesses reported that the horrors were unimaginable. Everything was on fire, the sky was red, homes all in flames. Children were running out on the street while still on fire. The river was full of corpses and the smell of napalm filled the air. "Babies were burning on the backs of parents. Animals were on fire, too," recalled a witness named Nihei for a CNN interview in 2020. (She is one of the few remaining survivors, aged 83 at the time of the interview).

Major General LeMay is widely quoted as saying, "Killing Japanese didn't bother me very much at that time... I suppose if I had lost the war, I would have been tried as a war criminal." LeMay was never tried for war crimes, but he was awarded numerous medals and later promoted to lead the US Strategic Air Command.

The non-atomic bombing attacks have been largely overlooked while teaching about WWII and are commonly overshadowed by discussions of the atomic bombs. Tokyo was not the only city that was set ablaze. The carnage was deemed so effective, the strategy was used on other major cities like Osaka, Kobe and Nagoya; followed by 58 "medium sized towns" killing tens of thousands more people along the way. Those campaigns set a military precedent for targeting civilian areas that persisted into the Korean and Vietnam wars that followed.

A Lesson in Empathy from My High School History Teacher

I remember talking about Tokyo in school. I was fortunate to have an insightful history teacher who cautioned us to pay close attention to the stories on the periphery. She asked us to drop the labels of axis and allies for a moment and imagine how we would feel if a foreign nation dropped bombs on our civilian population centres.

She asked us to imagine waking up to a sky on fire, everything we know and love turning to ash. She reminded us that every one of those people had dreams and hopes; they were somebody's mother, father, uncle, aunt, brother, sister or child. They loved and were loved. It was one of the greatest lessons in empathy I ever experienced in school.

She pointed out that iconic events make it into the movies, but many real experiences and people on the margins throughout time have been left off the pages of history. We collectively need to keep their stories alive too

Rude Awakening

Published by Seeking Veritas on Substack: Jun 6, 2023

On August 28th, 1963, Martin Luther King Jr delivered his now-famous "I have a Dream" speech on the steps of the Lincoln Memorial. A quarter million people had gathered in the American capital to hear him, and as always, the Reverend spoke with eloquence; he stirred emotions, ignited the flames of belief, and encouraged a people to keep the hope for change alive. The speech was a watershed moment; it would be spoken of, quoted, and taught for decades to come, not only in the United States but all over the world.

Sixty years later, though, as the concepts of diversity, equity and inclusion (DEI) are front and centre in the cultural conversation, it may be tempting to assume that King would feel joy and delight at how far we've come. But not so fast — that assumption would prove naive at best. If we unpack the nuances of DEI and what it has become, we're forced to come to the unfortunate conclusion that King, if he were to wake up in 2023, would be in for a rude awakening; that is, in the name of racial justice, we've returned to a segregation of sorts.

Inclusivity, indeed, is the trend of the times — the zeitgeist, so to say, the adult equivalent of the cool kids' table at the cafeteria. We give it a great deal, if not too much, prominence in our cultural discourse. But we know, as our high school days teach us, that the cool kids aren't popular because of objective merits; popularity works in very strange ways, especially in the minds of the young. Worse still, when the cool kids gang together and succumb to groupthink, which they almost always do, the bullying is relentless, and someone must stand on the receiving end of the vicious attacks.

John McWhorter, a vocal critic of simplistic DEI policies, describes in his book Woke Racism three waves of anti-racist activism. Granted, he speaks primarily to the black experience in America, but his point is transferable. The first wave of anti-racist activists, he argues, battled slavery and legalized segregation. The second wave, through the 70s and 80s, battled racist attitudes and demonstrated the moral flaw in racism. The third wave, he posits, became mainstream in the 2010s and teaches that because racism is baked into the structure of society, everyone who fails to denounce it is complicit by living within it. A central feature of this anti-racist activism wave, according to McWhorter, is that for marginalized groups, racism forms the totality of their lived experience. Focused on hyper-inclusivity of all marginalized people, the third wave of anti-racist activism considers everyone who disagrees to be either acting from privilege or ignorance. McWhorter refers to this new wave of activism as almost religious in their zeal and fervour.

For some, diversity is all about identifying the structural forces that have marginalized people. For others, it serves as a means of seeking retributive justice designed to assign blame, create shame, and elevate the voices of those previously marginalized regardless of their perspective or position. The latter is commonly debated in popular media and everyday interactions. At times, we call it virtue signalling; at others, we refer to it as being woke.

The reality is, regardless of what we choose to call it, this is a deeply divisive phenomenon. As we look back at the dark history that made DEI necessary in the first place, it's impossible to stay blind to the fact that retributive justice has a fundamentally othering influence. What's more, it redraws the old, dividing lines between racial groups that we seek to do without. Inequities cause harm and hurt, and the wounds run deep to this day, but we must ask ourselves, do two wrongs really make a right? This, I think, is the question we must face, because what we've come to call inclusivity does not look inclusive at all and raises many questions.

Why does there appear, for instance, and despite all attempts at inclusivity-based reforms, to be a widening chasm between white people and BIPOC (black, indigenous and people of colour) folk? The common and simplistic explanation we hear is that white people are merely resisting the demand to surrender power and privilege, and the discomfort they experience is an inevitable by-product of being called out. But not all white people are considered equal. Membership to the group deemed white has varied with time. Italian, Irish, Scottish and Eastern European people did not neatly fit into the dominant group of "white" at various stages of history.

Moreover, why does inclusivity, for all its good intentions, create such deep fracture lines within the group it seeks to elevate? Many, after all, are the BIPOC critics who refute simplistic DEI practices, retributive justice, and the politics of division. But in this case, the answer is made obvious by asking another question: why are some families — people who, remember, are genetically related — torn by political and religious disagreements? Perhaps, just perhaps, race and ethnicity alone don't define a person, just as race and ethnicity does not create monolithic groups that think, feel and opine the same way. And perhaps, just perhaps, we need to accept the broad nature of diversity; that it encompasses not only race, gender and sexuality, but also politics, thoughts, and opinions.

We don't need to travel very far to see that liberals and conservatives populate every demographic, and that oppression can strike any group. Limiting diversity to race, gender and sexuality only means the end of individual identity — the removal of our very humanity — and makes our understanding of inclusion myopic. Why, after all, would a black, indigenous, or any other person of colour be condemned for not believing in the commonly accepted notion of inclusivity? Why would that make them less brown, less black, or less indigenous?

Some of the core questions raised by DEI and woke ideology include: are we assigning priority based on degrees of suffering? If we are, who gets to decide how much suffering and how much privilege a person and their history has endured or enjoyed? Seen from this vantage point, the common vernacular of inclusivity is being utilized to divide rather than include. The focus on a common humanity is missing in the discourse of inclusivity.

Andrew Sullivan, in a 2018 New York Magazine article, argues that our problems are compounded when we insist that only a minority can speak about racism or homophobia:

> *"The only reason this should be the case is if we think someone's identity is more important than the argument, they might want to make... in this Orwellian world, some groups are more equal than others... So, if you wonder why our discourse is now so frightened with fear, why so many choose silence as the path of least resistance... The goal of our culture now is not the emancipation of the individual from the group, but the permanent definition of the individual by the group. We used to call this bigotry. Now we call it being woke."*

To trade individual rights for group rights, it goes without saying, is social and political regression. At least it should be obvious in our part of the world. Today western countries have moved from monarchical regimes to liberal and democratic systems in which the individual is supreme. This very individualism gave birth to our modern notion of human rights and guarantees the level of legal equality we've earned over the past 60 years. To assume that any variance in outcomes must solely be an outgrowth of historical subjugation flies in the face of individual agency, capacity, and choice; and borders on a dangerous notion of determinism. And if the consequence for dissenting against a tyrannical majority is career suicide, social ostracism, or general de-platforming, self-censorship becomes the prevailing modus operandi — and censorship of any form is illiberal.

We seem to have lost sight of the undeniable notion that active dissent is necessary for progress. Fredrick Douglass said it best. "Liberty," he argued, "is meaningless where the right to utter one's thoughts and opinions has ceased to exist." Yet for so many people, the simple thought of talking about racism is uncomfortable to the point of making self-censorship preferable. Why is it so uncomfortable? Perhaps because the conversation around racism isn't inclusive, because not everyone can see themselves in the conversation. There used to be a time when we fought for the removal of labels, of reductive identities, of being labelled by the colour of our skin and divided by superficial racial characteristics. Today, these labels seem at the forefront of all we discuss, and terrifyingly, it is moving into the realm of social reality again.

According to FIRE (Foundation for Individual Rights and Expression), several U.S. universities and colleges have hosted events, sponsored or promoted by minority advocates that make identity politics a central feature of their mission and purpose. Harvard University reserved an exclusive space for Black-identifying audience members at a performance of a reimagining of Macbeth, and Georgetown University's Campus Ministry held a meditation event whose description suggested it was exclusively for black students. It also hosted an event titled The Cookout, promoted with an advertisement describing the event as "created by Black students for Black students." These are only some examples of the changing zeitgeist.

At New York University (NYU), students began a petition calling on the administration to designate racially segregated housing for black and black-identifying students. At Western Washington University, black-only student housing was set up under a program called Black Affinity Housing. The University of Nevada, Las Vegas offers special race-based housing as well. The University of California, Berkeley, meanwhile, offers four orientations based on race in addition to the main orientation. Portland State University holds meetings "solely for people of color." In fact, more than seventy-five colleges across America now offer separate graduation ceremonies based on race, ethnicity, or sexual identity.

In Canada, Toronto's Metropolitan University (TMU), formerly Ryerson University, responded to community feedback with the creation of The Black Student Lounge (BSL). The lounge, the university's website describes, was created to:

> "... provide an intentional and affirming space on campus where Black students, across intersections, can feel a sense of belonging at the university... a safe space on campus for Black students, by Black students... Black-identifying students can access the lounge to study, relax, make new friends, gain tools and resources, build community and heal from the exhaustion of navigating systemic racism in their day to day lives. In this room, Black students are reminded that they exist beyond their trauma and oppression. Although this is primarily a student-centred space, Black faculty and staff at TMU are also welcome."

Harmela Kassa, an organizing member of the University of British Columbia's (UBC) Black Student Union, says that being black on campus can often lead to feelings of alienation, especially if you're also an international student. In an interview, Kassa says the organization is pushing for UBC to help develop a black space on campus for black students. According to Kassa, "There is a demand. There is an audience. There are black students on this campus who need a space, who want a space to connect with other black students on campus, and we need to facilitate that." UBC's vice-president reported working with students to identify such a space.

In response to editorials and news stories discussing what appears to many as re-segregation, the NYU independent student newspaper provided a response in an article they titled "Providing Safe Spaces for Black Students Does Not Mean Segregation":

"Claiming that white people are being segregated when Black students request a space where they can feel safe and supported not only misrepresents the reality of what NYU is doing but overlooks the institutional racism that leads Black students to need a supportive space in the first place. There is a difference between a privileged group oppressing another group of people by excluding them from spaces due to race and a marginalized community asking for a space where they can find support. The argument that this is segregation only further shows that the nuances and history of systemic racism are still being completely, if not willfully ignored by many."

On the other end of the debate, a USA Today op-ed writer posited:

> *"It was the argument of the old-time segregationists that the various races were too different to get along side by side. The best that could be hoped for was that each could stay in its lane and flourish on its own with minimal contact with the others. That's sounding more and more like the sort of thing we're hearing on college campuses, where each group is told that others can't understand its thinking because of its unique experiences, requiring its own safe space."*

Depending on your point of view, you may agree with one of the two positions above. You may also choose some middle ground in between, though that space is quickly disappearing before our eyes.

Anyone who has ever heard me speak knows where I stand on the phrase "people of colour." I still fail to see the distinction between that and the former normative expression, "coloured person." I have been called a Paki, a sand-nigger, a raghead and a camel jockey, yet I choose to not let those pejorative descriptions define me. I am glad we are making progress everyday. I am glad that my bi-racial child will most likely never have someone throw a coffee at him, call him a Paki, or tell him to go back to where he came from. Is life perfect now? Far from it. But the history of the world has never been fair. And I, for one, think it is time to stop letting perfection be the enemy of the good. I don't suggest that every person must accept my position. I personally find comfort, however, in that quote often attributed to Martin Luther King Jr.:

"The arc of the moral universe is long, but it bends towards justice."

Or perhaps I am just the wrong kind of coloured person. The pesky agitator always questioning, always challenging, always trying to get to the root. Perhaps I simply bemoan simple narratives and reductive binaries; I believe they fail to capture the inherent complexity of life, relying too heavily on the old and tired good-or-evil trope.

For example, the vacuous nature of woke philosophy was on full display after the unfortunate killing of Tyre Nichols. As is now standard practice, a debrief session was held in the aftermath of the news story reaching Canadian media. To assist people in dealing with what they read, a couple of special guest speakers were brought in to discuss the incident and examine why it keeps happening to black people. For added support, they also brought in someone to speak about black mental health. I asked an attendee what their takeaway was, and the answer I received was that systemic racism is so prevalent in policing that the white supremacists in this case were the five black officers who killed Tyre Nichols.

The woke almost seem like the good coloureds of yesteryear, because what they offer is palatable — groupthink that satisfies our impulse for martyrdom and promises rebirth in the great awakening. In this narrative, white people receive a mea culpa moment if they can attest to being racists, either consciously or subconsciously. Us coloureds should find vindication in the fear we can create by the mere suggestion that the bonds of slavery and subjugation are still ever present, despite laws dictating the contrary.

People are more comfortable today with accepting a generalized type casting of coloured mental health, spaces reserved for coloured people, and programming for coloured people that shields us from the ubiquitous white knowledge on offer in academic institutions. How ironic given the struggle endured to tear down the systems of segregation. How ironic given the challenges to the doctrine of separate but equal. How ironic given the beating endured in Selma. And how ironic given that even George Wallace recanted and showed remorse for his infamous line, "Segregation Now, Segregation Tomorrow, Segregation Forever!" Maybe we all need to reflect on the words of Mr. Rodney King, who asked if we could all just get along.

Travelling the world has been a rich experience for me personally and made me appreciate the diversity of culture and tradition that characterizes so many different peoples. My life will always be richer for those experiences, and yet it constantly highlighted the tumultuous nature of social hierarchies. To have seen the beauty in diversity around the globe makes the effort to find common purpose and common humanity all the more worthwhile. I will conclude by yielding the floor to a far superior orator, one whose credibility is generally unquestioned, who towers above all others in the minds of people of colour everywhere. The contents of whose character should spare him from being cancelled posthumously (hopefully):

I must say to my people who stand on the warm threshold which leads into the palace of justice. In the process of gaining our rightful place, we must not be guilty of wrongful deeds. Let us not seek to satisfy our thirst for freedom by drinking from the cup of bitterness and hatred... We must not allow our creative protest to degenerate into physical violence... The marvellous new militancy which has engulfed the Negro community must not lead us to a distrust of all white people... Let us not wallow in the valley of despair, I say to you today, my friends. So even though we face the difficulties of today and tomorrow, I still have a dream... I have a dream that one day this nation will rise up and live out the true meaning of its creed: We hold these truths to be self-evident, that all men are created equal... I have a dream that one day on the red hills of Georgia, the sons of former slaves and the sons of former slave owners will be able to sit down together at the table of brotherhood... I have a dream that my four little children will one day live in a nation where they will not be judged by the color of their skin but by the content of their character. I have a dream today... that one day... little black boys and black girls will be able to join hands with little white boys and white girls as sisters and brothers... And when this happens... all of God's children, black men and white men, Jews and Gentiles, Protestants and Catholics, will be able to join hands and sing in the words of the old Negro spiritual: Free at last, free at last. Thank God Almighty, we are free at last.

When reading King's speech today, one really must wonder what he would make of our world. In the same spirit, United Nations representative and human rights activist Mohamad Safa famously said, "Our world is not divided by race, colour, gender or religion. Our world is divided into wise people and fools. And fools divide themselves by race, colour, gender or religion." There is no doubt that Martin Luther King Jr would see great progress in our 21st century awakening. But he would see in the woke movement the very opposite of his ideal... and probably find that awakening pretty rude.

Progressive Separatism Beyond the White Gaze

Published by Seeking Veritas on Substack: May 7, 2024

On February 17, 2023, the National Arts Centre (NAC) hosted its first-ever "Black Out" night at Ottawa's Babs Asper Theatre, with a black-only performance of Is God Is, by playwright Aleshea Harris, about two black sisters.

"Black Out" is a movement that started in 2019 with the Broadway comedy Slave Play by playwright Jeremy O. Harris. According to the movement's website, "A

BLACK OUT is the purposeful creation of an environment in which an all-Black-identifying audience can experience and discuss an event in the performing arts, film, athletic, and cultural spaces — free from the white gaze." In his opening remarks for Slave Play, Harris encouraged the audiences to laugh, talk back and to be full participants in the experience of his play.

The white gaze is a term popularized by critically acclaimed writer Toni Morrison. When describing how it operates, Morrison said that it's this idea that "[Black] lives have no meaning and no depth without the white gaze." In the simplest terms, the white gaze can be conceptualized as the assumed white reader. When writers craft stories, the assumed white (and often cisgender, heterosexual, male) audience that they are writing for and to is the white gaze in action. The white gaze can be expanded to mean the ways in which whiteness dominates how we think and operate within society. Being encouraged to adhere to white-centered norms and standards is one of the ways that the white gaze operates. – Forbes, December 28, 2021

The National Arts Centre was accused of planning a racially segregated show and faced media and community backlash as a result. In response, the NAC released a statement emphasizing that their intention was to create a special evening for the black community, but would operate on an honour system of self identification. They emphasized that no one would actually be barred from entering, but they wanted the event to be true to the spirit of other "Black Out" events.

The decision to not enforce the entry intention may have been legally prudent rather than moralistic or principled, as it would have served to mitigate or minimize potential legal action. Any potential legal challenge risked the possibility of finding its way to the Supreme Court of Canada, where a ruling against it would be a major setback for the progressive separatism movement currently on the rise across North America.

Progressive separatism is an ideology that posits individuals are not much more than part of a group, either privileged or oppressed. It advocates for identity-based policies as a means of addressing historical inequities.

The strategy to not legally prevent access but rather let social pressure create alienation is actually one of the recommendations on the Black Out movement's website. On the home page of the website, they ask and answer the questions, "How did you make it clear that the performance was for Black-identifying individuals?" and "How is this legally accomplished?" The advice they offer is as follows:

- Keep the performances private and by invitation-only.
- Take tickets off-sale and make them only available for
purchase using a special code.
- Send the code to select organizations that support the
cause.
- Do not actively or officially prevent, preclude, or turn
away anybody from attending the BLACK OUT
performances.

The last point is interesting and was either adopted or
also naturally arrived at by the NAC. By not actively
denying anyone entry they are arguably skirting Charter
rights guaranteed to all Canadians. It may be fair to
suggest that they were however coming perniciously
close to the line.

Being a person who doesn't self identify as black, I
cannot speak to the perceived social and cultural value of
the initiative. I'm not certain if the majority of the black
community support such initiatives, or necessarily agrees
that the encouragement to participate in the play by
talking back to the performers makes the experience
more authentically black, as Jeremy O. Harris appears to
imply. If I had to guess, I would think that age
demographics would be a highly predictive indicator
about which side of the issue people would fall on.
The premise of the "Black Out" movement shares
ideological similarities with Affinity Groups that are

increasingly more common in society today. Advocates of Affinity Groups argue that they are not segregationist but rather a place where white people can "reckon with their Whiteness" and non-white people can "take care of themselves and one another... in the absence of Whiteness."

Opponents of the ideology supporting Affinity Groups tend to ground their opposition in theories such as Gordon Allport's "contact hypothesis" which argues that prejudice and conflict between groups can be reduced if members of the groups interact with each other. The argument suggests that affinity groups create fertile grounds for affinity bias, the unconscious gravitation toward people similar to ourselves. Affinity bias could result in reinforcing in-group opinions and cultural beliefs. The lack of diversity could create an echo chamber in which people get limited to their own worldview, making them less empathetic.

While the contact hypothesis has been studied most often in the context of racial prejudice, researchers have found that contact was able to reduce prejudice against members of a variety of marginalized groups.
In his book The Identity Trap, Yascha Mounk argues that universalism is currently being undermined in the name of "progressive separatism." Mounk argues that telling people to continually focus on their identities prioritizes

difference and exacerbates divisions. He argues that "it is self-defeating to embrace the divisiveness of identity separatism and to somehow expect the age-old problems of in-group tribalism not to emerge with predictably devastating impacts on vulnerable minorities."

With the social temperature and tensions turned up it is hard to engage in rational discussion about such things, leaving people trapped in their own echo chambers searching for answers. Inevitably, apathy and self-defeat become the likely outcome where no common ground can be found. Apathy is possibly the most unfortunate outcome on issues that many feel so passionate about.

Regardless of whether you believe identity-based policies or universalist principles are the path to a better future, we shouldn't lose sight of the fact that we need to work together, because talking past each other is going to get us nowhere.

Brown Professor says, "If you see something, say something"

Published by Seeking Veritas on Substack: Jun 9, 2023

"Ignorance more often begets confidence than does knowledge."
– Charles Darwin

What does 9/11 have to do with DEI?

Following the terror attacks on the Word Trade Center on September 11, 2001, the New York Metropolitan Transportation Authority (NYMTA) implored every New

Yorker to report suspicious activities they saw on their network. The NYMTA went so far as to trademark the phrase, "If You See Something, Say Something®" to raise awareness of the signs of terrorism. Today, the phrase is even licensed by the Canadian Association of Chiefs of Police.

But while the "If You See Something, Say Something®" campaign had positive intent, it also came with a dark side. It created unwarranted paranoia, reductive labelling, and sweeping generalizations that only served to divide people. In the wake of the tragedy, our Muslim and Sikh brothers and sisters found themselves unfairly discriminated against by fellow citizens who chose the politics of divisiveness and vindication. Sikhs felt the wrath of prejudice because some people couldn't distinguish between turbans, while Muslims experienced the ignorant by-products of reducing approximately 1.3 billion people to a single label. More than twenty years later, we have normalized those othering stereotypes and the social justice activists have moved to the seemingly noble pursuit of Diversity, Equity, and Inclusion. Yet I can't help finding that DEI, for all its good intentions, has become a war on individuality. A war with unintended consequences like we saw 20 years ago.

I've been pondering these thoughts for some time, and sometimes I do wonder if I have a legitimate issue with common DEI training. Am I simply virtue signalling, too? In moments of self doubt I wonder if I am taking a position that goes against the normative diversity narrative merely to stand out. Perhaps it is hubris or a need to demonstrate the intellectual limitations of unquestioned conformity. Whatever the reason, I find myself engaging in this conversation more often recently, but why?

My opinions are informed by my lived experience which, in contemporary DEI parlance, should be enough to validate the truth of my perspective. But I have also been consuming vast amounts of information, perspectives, and insights informed by other people's lived experiences and philosophies. Among other authors, I have considered the works of Ibram X. Kendi, Ta-Nehisi Coates, and Robyn DiAngelo. I have layered in knowledge on offer by Robyn Maynard, Michelle Alexander, and Michael Eric Dyson; and I have balanced it with dissent from Irshad Manji, John McWhorter, Isabel Wilkerson, Randall Kennedy and Andrew Sullivan. Ironically, all of it has served to reinforce my appreciation for the quote commonly attributed to Darwin, "Ignorance more often begets confidence than does knowledge."

Indeed, the more often I discuss this topic, the more commonly I discover that people on both sides of the issue limit their reading selections to one worldview or the other. They rarely read from across the divide, which is required for serious intellectual enquiry and truth-seeking endeavours. One recent example found me particularly shocked. The school board my children attend was hosting an anti-black racism session, so I decided to attend. The speaker, an individual the school board visibly has a great deal of confidence in, spoke at the elementary school where my youngest child attends. The same individual also spoke at the high school my older children attend. Three aspects from the talk stood out to me, all of which felt extremely concerning.

The message was largely divisive; it highlighted many reasons why white members of the audience should feel shame and guilt. It offered a reductive and deterministic justification for any negative experiences of black and brown students, and it discounted any participatory role agency might have played. The speaker also made sure to pay lip service to signal inclusion of indigenous peoples, while saying nothing of substance regarding them. Equally troubling was that the speaker offered no suggestions that could help students bridge divides, find common respect or focus on future-forward community-building initiatives. Call me an extreme pragmatist, but I found myself biting my lips throughout the talk, as I saw nothing in that speech that would practically help us make our society better.

More concerning still, the speaker didn't take questions from parents or students. The customary Q&A session was non-existent. The issues being discussed, it was being signalled, were not to be questioned, nor were they to be critically engaged with. We should instead accept them as sacrosanct. The speaker went so far as to imply that there were only two options available: people could either admit they hold racist attitudes, or they should accept the fact that they are indeed racists because of their failure to recognize their failings. These were the only two options, and they both left me unsatisfied. In my work, I take the time to unpack the complexity of our human nature, and the speaker's explanations did not, in any way, do justice to the nuances and intricacies of our world.

The most glaring aspect of the presentation was the obvious one-sidedness. While the speaker frequently cited Kendi and DiAngelo, when pressed by parents about other scholars of colour like Manji, McWhorter, or Thomas Sowell, he promptly dismissed them, stating that he hated those books, and they weren't worth reading. It turns out that our school board endorses speakers who find comfort in their self-affirming echo chambers, refuse to face legitimate disagreements even through civil discourse, and fail to answer basic requirements of intellectual rigour. The speaker sponsored by the school board was, in effect, only that — a speaker. An ideologically driven sophist who paid lip service to vague, undefined notions of diversity, equity and inclusion but who did not bring anything valuable to the table.

At the end of the sessions, a few parents discussed how the talk ignored invaluable counterarguments that are easily discoverable and readily accessible in bestselling books like Don't Label Me. In it, Irshad Manji argued that those who advocate for diversity too often end up creating conformity in part due to their fixation on labeling. Labels, Manji maintains, drain diversity of its unifying potential. Similarly, John McWhorter, in Woke Racism, posits that much of the anti-racism ideology infantilizes black and brown people. It considers them as fragile and incapable of self-determination because it shows white people are their kryptonite. These two books among many others, despite being written by serious scholars of colour, failed to meet the speaker's ideological requirements. This, in today's climate, was good enough ground for dismissal. It didn't matter that the talk was about the fact that marginalization of any voice of a person of colour is tantamount to racism.

While the talk itself may have been disappointing, I did find a silver lining in the sky. Parents, who had been attentive to the talk, drew attention to the one-sided presentation, hardly the intellectual rigour our schools should be modelling if we hope to develop critical thinking in our children. Many parents did not buy into the ideological dogma brought by the speaker and pushed back on these notions they deemed unhelpful. However, some of them were happy to go along with the speaker's agenda. A parent who seemed particularly pleased about the speaker and his remarks interjected against the critics with an astounding comment that critical thinking and objective truth are examples of white supremacy and products of white hegemony. This position, surprisingly, is supported by the anti-racism movement and literature.

So why engage more nowadays? Back in the mid 2010s, when a small but vocal group of DEI/social justice activists started spreading a more divisive message, most moderate people of colour thought it was a phase that would pass. The extremes would get tempered, and the pendulum would return to the middle allowing for sensible discourse to return. We were wrong, as it turns out, and the new normal is now ubiquitous from educational institutions to the corporate sector. As a person of colour, I find myself unimpressed by people who purport to speak for me and for all people who look like me, as if we were one monolithic group who all think, feel and opine the same way.

Since I attended the event because of my kids, I couldn't help but ask myself this important and terrifying question: is my child, who is half brown and half white, also half oppressor and half oppressed? Does his white privilege overshadow his brown historical subjugation? Or does his brown historical subjugation overshadow his white privilege? And what about his mother? Is she inherently evil, a white devil? Am I, his father, inherently marginalized? What if I don't feel this way (even though, back in 1990s, I was called a "Paki and sand nigger," told to go back to where I came from, and had a Tim Hortons coffee thrown at me)? More importantly, how do I, as a father, help my child make sense of this world?

When we look at where DEI has taken us, it's easy to see that we've returned to the familiar, immediate post 9/11 social attitude. Racism is a real problem, and we have a right to be angry. But if, by trying to right the historical wrongs, we cause paranoia and divisiveness, are we actually accomplishing something? The policy for me has always been simple. If you see something, say something. And this is true for either type of divisiveness. If you see racism, say something. If you see divisiveness disguised as DEI, say something. And if you see someone lost in the divisive jargon of inclusivity, remind them of our common humanity.

If we ever hope to end racism and be a truly inclusive society, we need respect for our common humanity, even when we disagree. Respect for diversity of thought and opinion, even if our perspectives vary. Respect for personhood, that beautifully complex state of being that is so hard to reduce to a single label. And respect for community and for each other, with all the perfectly natural imperfections of our human experience. Because individuality still matters; divisiveness and determinism fail to celebrate the rich diversity that is the human condition.

The Problem of Race

Published by Seeking Veritas on Substack: May 28, 2024

"Race is the child of racism, not the father." – Ta-Nehisi Coates

Race is not a biological fact, but to many, it is a social reality. Race is the host upon which the parasitic monster Racism feeds. It's only over the last five centuries that race, as we understand it today, has become an organizing principle constructed socially, politically, and legally to structure societies, comprehend experiences, and develop identities. Race is the shorthand that allows

247

us to categorize the US and the THEM. But is it deterministic, unchanging, and eternal?

Should we nurture race, take pride in it, and hold on to it, or reform it? Should we celebrate the black experience and the brown experience? What about the white experience — is that a current social fact or merely a historical reference? How about the blended beige experience or the more ambiguous white-adjacent experience? Where do they fit on the cherished mountain of lived experiences? What wisdom might we access if we choose to imbibe from the sea of human experience instead?

Singularity
Regardless of whether you are a descendant from the Indus Valley, the Arabian desert, or Mount Something-Mythical, for all those who believe in a supreme deity — that omnipotent, omniscient, and omnipresent watchmaker — the origin of humankind has a singularity and a common, albeit divine source. A oneness, a masterpiece that reflects its creator. For some, the supreme deity with divine power created a goddess through whom the first human was born, who subsequently fathered the rest of humanity. Some insist that humans are a special creation built in the image of the divine. Others yet will offer that the supreme being

created the first human from clay and then breathed spirit into him.

For the secular science-y types, the great origin story began with apelike ancestors approximately six million years ago, which led to bipedalism, large complex brains, and ultimately the capacity for language. It involved a walking tour out of Africa into Asia, ultimately leading to Europe and eventually the Americas. Notice, however, that here too, the origin of humankind has a singularity and a common, albeit evolved source. A oneness, a masterpiece that reflects cause and effect, adaptation and variation.

For believers and non-believers alike, the accepted wisdom is that from one we became many. That point is worth repeating: FROM ONE WE BECAME MANY. Said differently, before we were many, we shared a common humanity, a foundational origin story grounded in singularity, a history of cooperation not just conflict, and a proliferation of life by multiplication not division. Moreover, regardless of a secular or religious disposition, history demonstrates a consistent human capacity for blending, adapting, and growing community, notwithstanding our other equally prolific proclivity for ostracism, retrenchment, and destruction. Our capacity for language allowed us to organize dominion over all other living beings, while ironically creating disharmonies among ourselves.

Racial Categories

According to the American Association of Biological Anthropologists (AABA):

"No group of people is, or ever has been, biologically homogeneous or 'pure', human populations have never been biologically discrete, isolated, or static… and there is significant scientific consensus that genetic variability within and among human groups does not follow racial lines."

There is a certain arbitrary and artificial division in what we understand today as race and therefore racial experience. The most damaging legacy of racial essentialism are the structures of inequality that have tainted the human experience, both past and present.

If five centuries of data, history, and yes, experience, has taught us that racial categorization is a by-product of prejudice, bias, hatred, and their corollary, racism, why do we cling so tightly to a construct that has done so much to undermine our common humanity? Race is not a biological fact, and yet we use it and embed it into our education system, our government, our workplaces, our policies, and our personal lives.

The Paradox

One may logically conclude that we have so deeply internalized the construct of race that the most critical among us see it as an inevitable social fact, immutable and eternal. However, once you arrive at that conclusion, you've boxed yourself into a paradox. Race is, at one and the same time, not real and also the source of the greatest injustice. From that vantage point you must fight the thing that both isn't there, and that is also consistently kicking your arse and holding you down. Of course, to not appear as merely a shadow boxer, you must commit to its existence, lest someone thinks you are simply fighting an imaginary enemy.

Let me be clear; we all do operate in a world that acts as if race is real, we design systems around the concept and order society as if it were true. But for the lie to work, it must be constant and unwavering. In the morning when the bigots arrive and speak of superiority and human hierarchies, you will fire back that we are all the same if only they could go further than skin deep. You will remind them that DNA proves that "between any two humans, the amount of genetic variation — biochemical individuality — is about 0.1 percent." In the evening however, when the agent of the state arrives, you will remind them of the historical marginalization and the need for special interest groups and race-based remedies. You will advocate for creating programs for the racially oppressed (at least those that can organize and enlist lobbyists). You will support targeted grants and funding models that support your uniquely selected racial group deemed deserving.

You may even articulate a reason why the money should flow to the equity-deserving before the equity-seeking groups — and definitely over the historically privileged, even if some of their members are currently impoverished. It appears there are great incentives for everyone to keep the concept of race intact. We really need to think about why we do that, and more importantly, how our fealty to the concept inhibits our ability to address racism where it exists.

The Prestige
So, is race the child of racism or the father? Are we so varied we must either fight or celebrate our difference, or do we originate from a singularity worth remembering? Do we have black, brown or white experiences or simply human experiences — experiences full of complexity, contradictions, and duality?

Perhaps I spend too much time philosophizing about an ideology whose tenets are already calcified, whose litmus test I cannot pass, whose dogma I cannot adopt, whose canonical doctrine I will not recite, and whose orthodoxy

I will not abide. Or maybe it's hubris that has made me believe I have any of this right.

I borrow, then bastardize, Hume's account of Epicurus when I ponder: if racism is evil and race its progeny, can we not stop it? If we are willing but not able, then we are impotent. If we are able but not willing, then we are malevolent. If we are both able and willing, then its continued existence is simply evidence of complicity, or worse, apathy. That's the generous reading; the alternative would be far more cynical, but dare I put Mark Antony's words in the mouths of the ideologues, who knowingly may utter, "Cry havoc and let slip the dogs of war," for time and time again we have seen that there is a predictable, albeit contrived order that comes after chaos, regardless if that chaos originated organically or by design.

I could say to hell with it, let the devil take tomorrow, but conformity has always been so damn boring!

Perceived Threats, Real Consequences

Published by Seeking Veritas on Substack: Jun 12, 2023

"This idea of purity and you're never compromised, and you're always politically 'woke' and all that stuff. You should get over that quickly. The world is messy; there are ambiguities. People who do really good stuff have flaws. People who you are fighting may love their kids and share certain things with you. There is this sense sometimes that the way of making change is to be as judgmental as possible about other people, and that's enough. That's not activism. That's not bringing about change. If all you're doing is casting stones, you're probably not going to get that far. That's easy to do." – Barack Obama 2019

An alleged hate motivated incident occurred at 12:30 p.m. on May 17, 2023, at a DriveTest Centre in Kitchener, Ontario. The incident was recorded and posted on the alleged victim's social media account by 2:55 p.m. the same day; police arrested the alleged offender by 10 p.m. At 10:18 p.m. the story was in local papers, and by 6:15am the next morning, articles were updated to include comments from local politicians. Mayor Cam Guthrie of Guelph, Ontario commented on the actions of the victim, saying, "You're very brave and powerful to call out such vile discrimination against you and others that were in that room." Within 24 hours the alleged victim, while being interviewed by media, called on the Federal government to establish a national support fund for survivors of hate.

Some people may feel rightful vindication and pride at how efficiently the system rallied to address such vile discrimination, as Mayor Guthrie characterized it. However, the pace of condemnation and resolution should give us reason to pause and prompt some further reflection.

The alleged victim reportedly overheard a generalized rude comment about brown people which contained an expletive. After canvassing if others heard it too, she chose to confront the person. The video available online shows her holding her phone camera and saying to the alleged offender, "Really you are going to be racist here in the Drive Test." Most news stories begin quoting the victim at her next line, which was, "I just said don't be rude. I didn't say anything else. We're all waiting in this line. Everybody heard you here making a racist comment about brown people."

What follows is undeniably an assault. The alleged offender is clearly seen striking the woman and throwing her phone. No reasonable argument supports her decision to use violence to deal with the situation. I do not condone it, nor argue in favour of it being justifiable.

While the alleged victim claims to be shocked that she was assaulted, there are some other factors worth considering. The alleged victim has stated on record that she works with the Waterloo Regional Police's equity diversity and inclusion unit as part of her job, with a local coalition that helps victims of this exact type of incident. She further reported that her active by-stander training promotes intervening from a safe distance, not physically engaging, and not provoking. Advice that was not heeded, as evidenced by her proximity when the alleged offender struck her.

The victim also reported that she called a member of the Waterloo Regional Police's equity diversity and inclusion unit for assistance right away; she stated she felt lucky to have the connections with the police that she did, as well as possessing an "understanding of how to handle these situations." The video seems to contradict that last statement. Which returns to my earlier comment about considering the facts and reflecting on the incident. By any objective measure the alleged offender did not present an imminent physical danger to the public or the victim. Her decision to utter the phrase "fucking brown people" in a public space demonstrates questionable judgement to be certain. Striking the victim was wrong regardless of how she was confronted about her poor social skills. But, given she did not present a physical danger, what was the motivation for the intervention and how was the bystander training followed?

Calling someone out as a racist, activates what best selling author and educator Irshad Manji refers to as the ego brain. That primitive part of us that is ruled by emotions; and the natural instinctive reaction is to lash back. Manji reminds us that "the problem is that the primal part of our brain cannot distinguish between mortal danger and mere discomfort." Being pragmatic requires us to know that sometimes the best strategy to deal with ugliness, or bigotry, is to recognize when we need to walk away. According to Columbia University Professor John McWhorter, author of the best-selling book Woke Racism, calling someone a racist today is comparable to calling them a pedophile — a very pointed and defensive reaction is almost guaranteed to follow.

Within twenty-fours of the event, the alleged victim, along with the coalition she works for, spoke to the media and called for the federal government to number one make good on its commitment to establish a national support fund for survivors of hate; and number two, develop new hate crime legislation. They also called on the provincial government to deliver an anti-racism strategy requiring social service agencies to provide regular training on anti-racism. The Chief Operating Officer of the coalition added that "The incident also draws our attention to the need for diversity, equity, inclusivity training for all public and private organizations that serve the community." A service their organization provides within the community where the incident took place.

Politicians may wish to be more judicious in what they call brave and powerful. One could look charitably at the actions of the alleged victim and decide she was merely acting with good intent, trying to spare others from hearing offensive comments. However, when local politicians praise such interventions, they may be seen as advocating for others to do the same. Such a recommendation could put people at real risk of physical harm if they are ill prepared when someone lashes back.

The police undergo extensive training in investigations, verbal de-escalation and defensive tactics; perhaps we need to let the police do what they are trained for. Citizens should absolutely do their part by calling 9-11 for active threats, and the non-emergency number when there is no imminent threat to safety and security.

For your additional consideration:

- I write this as an opinion editorial and only have access to information in the public domain. My opinion has been formulated based on the available information as reported in media stories and interviews, and the actions visible in the video.
- I refer to the woman who was assaulted as "the alleged victim" because I choose not to draw any unnecessary attention to her identity.
- This is not intended to "victim blame" or otherwise disparage her personhood. It is intended to objectively evaluate the direct facts and statements utilizing the primary evidence as supplied by the primary subject herself.
- I refer to the offender with the common addition of the word "alleged" because that is standard convention when referring to someone who has been accused or charged but not yet convicted. As a logical follow through, the crime is also alleged given she

has not been convicted. I do not intend to diminish her actions or the severity of the charges.

Colour Blindness: The Complication of a Simple Metaphor

Published by Seeking Veritas on Substack: Oct 3, 2023

"To interpret the phrase colour blindness literally is to misunderstand it. It uses a physical metaphor to capture an abstract idea. To advocate for colour blindness is not to pretend you don't notice race, it is to support a principle that we should try our best to treat people without regard to race both in our personal life and in our public policy." – Coleman Hughes

The news stories regarding Coleman Hughes' TED Talk made me ponder the reaction and response that has become fairly common anytime the phrase "colour blindness" comes up. I remember sensitivity training courses in the 90s that promoted the idea based on the seemingly sound logic that reducing a person to their immutable superficial characteristics was flawed. I guess we've evolved on that position in the second decade of the 21st century.

Hughes has spoken consistently on the subject of race and policy and as such, the content of his talk should not have come across as a surprise to anyone. He is an extremely intelligent, articulate and successful young social commentator who writes and communicates with refreshing clarity.

In an article Hughes wrote for The Free Press titled "Why Is TED Scared of Color Blindness?" he described his experience with TED the day after delivering his talk, "A Case for Color Blindness." He argued that the TED organization tried to suppress his talk after receiving complaints from a group called "Black@TED", an "Employee Resource Group that exists to provide a safe space for TED staff who identify as Black." However, when Hughes agreed to speak with the group and hear their concerns, Chris Anderson, the head of TED, informed him that Black@TED actually was not willing to speak with him.

When I did my TEDx Talk in Toronto in 2022, I called it "How Common Humanity Gets Lost in the Jargon of Inclusivity." One of the key components I discussed was our reductive use of labels to signal compliance with the racial nomenclature of the day. I specifically took issue with the term BIPOC, an acronym I personally think sounds like a disease. I am neither famous nor as popular as Coleman Hughes, but in my small way, I was trying to speak to the intent behind a colour-blind approach to social interactions. In the Talk, I mentioned that over the last several years, the acronym BIPOC (as in black, Indigenous, and people of colour) was perhaps intended to prioritize those previously marginalized and elevate their voices in an attempt to level the playing field.

Let's break that down. We are identifying the plight of black people on the basis of their history and suffering. We are identifying the current circumstances of Indigenous peoples on the basis of their history with colonialism and their suffering. We then lump everyone else who is not white, black or Indigenous into a single collective group with no identifiable history or story as "People of Colour." Is that inclusive or convenient? I suggest we have employed a certain degree of my-side bias, focused on recent activism, and then attempted to craft an all-encompassing narrative around it. Language can be divisive, and at the risk of splitting hairs, how do we decide who gets first billing? Why not indigenous first? They are, after all, the first peoples of this land.

Why are black people and indigenous peoples, distinct from other people of colour? Surely nobody believes that all the other people of colour have so insignificant a history on this continent that they are unworthy of distinction. Why are white people not people who could have been marginalized? To decide that all people of colour or all white people are a singular monolithic group that share characteristics so broad that specificity and distinction is not required, seems to violate the basic tenets of inclusivity.

The focus on a common humanity is missing in the discourse of inclusivity. It may be worth remembering that not all white people have always been considered equal. Membership to the group deemed white has also varied with time. Italian, Irish, Scottish and Eastern European people did not neatly fit into the dominant group of 'white' at various stages of history. Privilege in this context quickly becomes a matter of subjective evaluation.

Perhaps race and ethnicity alone do not define a person, nor make them all one monolithic group that all think, feel and opine the same way. Perhaps we need to accept that diversity of thought and opinions, just like the diversity of identifying variables, cannot be captured in such narrow terms. Freddie Deboer, writing for The Free Press, asks a critical question worth pondering: "What is the political value of dividing up progressive constituencies into smaller and smaller groups? How does that help anyone achieve any of their specific aims, including BIPOC people?"

Inclusivity today is a topic that is given a great deal of priority and prominence in our discourse. For some, it's practically about bringing previously marginalized people into the fold; shedding the mistreatment of the past and opening up access to resources for all people. For others however, it is a means of seeking retributive justice, assigning blame, creating shame, and elevating the voices of those previously marginalized regardless of their perspective or position. The latter strategy has a fundamentally othering influence and actually fails to acknowledge the richness of diversity among all people.

Robert P. George, Professor of Jurisprudence at Princeton University, suggests that supporters of anti-racism have adopted an ideology rooted in condemnation of "liberal theories an approaches that propose formal equality and color-blindness in public policy as mere masks for institutional or structural (systemic) racism." The contemporary anti-racist perspective is informed in large part by the vision of Boston University's Ibram X. Kendi, author of the bestselling How to Be an Anti-Racist, whose popularity has soared since 2020. Kendi advocates for what he calls, "positive antiracist discrimination" as a remedy to past discrimination:

> "The only remedy to past negative racist discrimination that has produced inequity is present positive antiracist discrimination that produces equity. The only remedy to present negative racist discrimination toward inequity is future positive antiracist discrimination toward equity."
> — Ibram X. Kendi

I am not arguing that there have been no historical grievances. My argument is also definitely not an endorsement of past inequities, but it should prompt us to question whether two wrongs do really make a right. Is social inclusion for some and not for all? Is common humanity limited to those previously commonly subjugated? And is there a way forward that celebrates our common humanity by learning from the lessons of history, that clearly demonstrates the flaws in assigning hierarchy by race or other features that are only skin deep? What happened to the desire to be judged by the content of our character rather than the colour of our skin?

To follow Kendi's advice would be to live in a constant state of cyclical discriminatory behaviour, while merely substituting who we consider the oppressor and the oppressed. Although I imagine that the Centre for Anti-Racist Research would argue that those categories are eternally fixed.

In his essay titled "Actually, Color-Blindness Isn't Racist", Hughes cites some of the early references to the phrase before it became a lightening rod in the culture debates of our times. Specifically, he draws attention to the positive use of the phrase "colour-blind" by several prominent individuals and highlighted that though it has roots in the Enlightenment, the color-blind principle was really developed during the fight against slavery and refined during the fight against segregation. See excerpts from the original article below:

- Wendell Phillips, the President of the American Anti-Slavery Society — in 1865, Philips called for the creation of "a government color-blind," by which he meant the total elimination of all laws that mentioned race. George Lewis Ruffin, America's first black judge, described Wendell Phillips as "wholly color-blind and free from race prejudice."
- The 1896 Supreme Court case Plessy vs. Ferguson — in his lone dissent, Justice John Marshall wrote,

"Our constitution is color-blind, and neither knows nor tolerates classes among its citizens."
- Justice John Marshall's statement on the constitution being color-blind was cited by NAACP lawyer Thurgood Marshall when he battled segregation in the courts.
- Among the main goals of the Civil Rights Movement was the elimination of laws and policies that used the category of race in any way — championed by Rev. Martin Luther King Jr.

A recent Angus Reid Institute survey on racism in Canada demonstrated that there is a perceptual gap between government, academia, and the population on whose behalf they are trying to fight systemic racism and oppression. "Currently the terms 'racialized minority' or 'racialized groups' or 'people of colour' are preferred by people labelled as visible minorities," reads one of several "anti-racism lexicons" now maintained by federal agencies. However, among non-white Canadians outside of government and academia, almost nobody is referring to themselves by the government-approved names for their demographic. A mere 6% of non-white Canadians polled used the terms racialized and BIPOC to describe themselves. Most people of colour, as we apparently like to be called, actually prefer the term "visible minority" according to the poll.

I leave you with three suggestions for consideration:

1. Perhaps our laws and our policies should focus on consistency of application and clarity of purpose rather than specificity of superficial differences.

2. We shouldn't need a reminder, but the dictionary definition of a metaphor is a figure of speech in which a word or phrase is applied to an object or action to which it is not literally applicable. So, when one says colour blindness, they do not mean literally that they cannot see race/colour.

3. We should narrow the gap between government policy, academic jargon, and the people who experience the actual issues in the community. Sometimes there really is value in keeping it simple and not over complicating every aspect of life!

The Social Pendulum

Published by Seeking Veritas on Substack: Jun 16, 2023

"Every action has an equal and opposite reaction."
– Issac Newton

Wokeism versus viewpoint diversity doesn't have the same catchy ring as "Thrilla in Manila" or "Rumble in the Jungle" but their respective constituencies often battle each other with comparable conviction and die-hard determination. What fuels the fire in their bellies? In this article, I suggest our social division is not about differing world views. Rather, it is inextricably linked to the inevitable ebb and flow of the social pendulum, based on our reactions to globalization and populism.

When Rodney King intervened with his famous question, "Can't we all just get along?" he was attempting to interrupt the Los Angeles Riots of 1992. As a result of several days of rioting, more than 50 people were killed, more than 2,300 were injured, and thousands were arrested. About 1,100 buildings were damaged, and total property damage was about $1 billion, which made the riots one of the most-devastating civil disruptions in American history. The thirty-year history following those riots have answered his question about whether we can get along with a resounding "apparently not!"

No Demilitarized Zones
Fewer people seem to be asking that question each year. There is a ubiquitous state of polarization that we seem to have internalized and normalized. The famous question has been altered into an opening statement, "Why we can't get along...", followed by detailed argumentation (ranging from logical to fantastical) justifying our divisions. By dropping and swapping a couple of words, the entire focal point of Rodney King's question shifts.

Good intentions, unchecked and unbalanced can have dire consequences and can rapidly become counterproductive. Our ideological allegiances reinforce the "us versus them" dichotomy, and somewhere along the way we stopped listening. We became content with speaking at instead of to each other. We gave up on dialogue in favour of monologues. We just stopped trying to get along.

A lot has been written about the plight of marginalized people, and a growing body of work is emerging to challenge the grand narrative often dubbed, being woke. I will not re-litigate the matter here. Regardless of where you stand, what is becoming increasingly evident is that there are no demilitarized zones in this conflict. Everyone is expected to take a side.

Global Villages & Citizens
What if the whole twenty-first century race and culture wars, in North America and Western Europe, are really a microcosm of a global pattern that has played out several times throughout history?

In the late eighties, the Cold War ended. The iron curtain collapsed, and the Berlin Wall was smashed. The well-known post WWII enemy was vanquished, and a global humanitarian worldview took hold. In the period between Hitler and Bin Laden, major social advances were tangibly achieved. Nation states gained independence from their colonizers. Religious tolerance improved; gender inequities were finally being addressed in meaningful ways; diversity within sexuality was acknowledged; widespread legalization finally prevented people from being prosecuted because of who they loved; civil rights legislation was passed; and racial animus was reduced. Technological advances made information more accessible and connected parts of the world previously knowable only by means of your high school atlas. The terms "global village" and "global community" became more common.

As people and business started travelling around this global village, jobs migrated, global labour markets opened, and the other side of inclusion slowly became apparent. Everyone was happy when the Indian and Chinese factories sent over their low-priced merchandise (which is awesome unless you ruin it by thinking too long about why the products are cheap). But then those people from third world countries thought, "if they like the things we make, they will probably like us too," and that's where the wheels fell off!

Rise of Populism
Globalization was all the rage until it wasn't. All of sudden, foreign-born people were in your neighbourhood, not just on your shirt labels. Folks in Pleasantville puckered, and a return to isolationism started looking like a really good political strategy.

Satire aside, over the last couple of decades global politics has trended universally away from liberalism. Think about all the countries whose populist parties either won elections or made major gains: Brazil, Venezuela, Poland, Hungary, Turkey, India, Philippines, France, Russia, Germany, Australia, and the United States, among many others. The rise of populism can be attributed to the fact that a global economy arguably benefits poor workers in developing countries and the 1% in advanced economies far more than it does the working and middle classes. Combine that economic reality with mass immigration and you have the recipe for nationalism and an "us versus them" attitude towards anyone who appears different.

The result is a perceived loss of status among former majorities.

> "As human experience suggests (and behavioural economists confirm) the pain of loss exceeds the pleasure of gain. While failing to improve one's well-being is despairing, losing ground is bitter... As demography shifts, 'old stock' citizens fear a loss of status and cultural centrality."– William A. Galston, Anti-Pluralism

Tribalism, an inherent feature of the human condition, becomes an easy answer. In-group solidarity increases, and people tend to exaggerate the differences between themselves and newer citizens.

After the Cold War, the emergence of India and China on the world stage added hundreds of millions of new workers to the global economy. Soon, those global citizens would start to travel; and soon, they would become the "other."

An Alternative Theory

"Those that fail to learn from history are doomed to repeat it."
– Winston Churchill (1948)

The pendulum always swings back. The further in one direction it goes the further it eventually swings the other way. If this is true, then we can see our social context in a new light:

- Imperialism motivates the desire for freedom.
- Freedom inevitably creates inequities.
- Inequities promote a desire for socialism.
- Socialism breeds despotism.
- Despotism is combatted by liberalism.
- Liberalism opens global communities.
- Global communities create global citizens.
- Global citizens increase the labour supply and immigration.
- Increased immigration threatens social status.

- A challenge to social status gives birth to populism.
- Populism leads to nationalism.
- Nationalism leads to tribalism.
- Tribalism requires an US and a THEM.

By the time anyone realized they were stuck in a loop propped up by simplistic binary thinking, the battle lines were drawn. Being woke, escalating social protests, race based social justice activism, and a reliance on group identity may just have been a response to the global shift to the right. However, whenever drastic shifts occur, they have the potential to produce an extreme response. Which begs the question, what happens next? If we cannot all just get along, perhaps we can expand the Overton Window to make room new policies that do not rely so heavily on polarization.

Perhaps we can find common humanity even among those we disagree with.

A Better DEI Path: Strong Voices and Unique Ideas to Reduce Divisiveness in Diversity Discourse

Published by Seeking Veritas on Substack: Dec 5, 2023

I have always believed that letting people speak freely was the best way to know where they stand on an issue. Silencing people does not change their negative attitudes, it merely masks or hides them. People have often asked how I feel when I hear racist or vile comments. My answer is simple: I do not let it rent space in my head.

277

My self-worth is not contingent on the musings of ignorant or bigoted people.

As a general rule of thumb, not letting stupidity rent space in my head has worked really well for me. That is not to imply that certain comments or attitudes don't make me cringe. I have plenty of thoughts on the veracity of prejudiced truth claims; they just don't make it very high on my list of priorities on any given day. But every now and again, the clickbait styled headline of a story stops me in my tracks. I know I should probably scroll on before getting unnecessarily vexed — but alas, occasionally I take the bait.

Is it clickbait if it's true?
On November 26th, 2023 — yes, I said 2023 -— I came across an article in the Wall Street Journal titled "To Shrink Learning Gap, This District Offers Classes Separated by Race" by Sara Randazzo and Douglas Belkin. After reading the article, I had to question my long-held belief that letting people speak freely is the best way to know where they stand on an issue. In 2023, I find it increasingly difficult to tell who the pro-segregationists are. The white sheets of yesteryear were so much simpler to pick out; sometimes they even signaled their bigotry with clear, albeit crude and uncouth, symbols like a burning cross.

Is it better to be with your own?

According to the article, the school district leaders in Evanston, just north of Chicago Illinois, were contending with an academic achievement gap in their district. Apparently when grades were analyzed based on students' identified race, they found disparities. Black and Latino students scored lower on standardized tests than white students. The school board believed race was the single most impactful variable that influenced performance, so they offered new classes at the high school voluntarily separated by race. (The enrolment had to be voluntary because federal law in the US prohibits public schools from utilizing mandatory segregation by race.)

In addition to segregating students by race, they found some research that indicated some small improvements could be found in grades, retention, and graduation rates if students were also taught by teachers of the same race. The approach included segregated options in core subjects like math and english. The article did not report on the success of the programs, but I anticipate that removing all the privileged higher-grade hoarders in the class would have impacted the class average and reduced the inequitable grade distribution.

Randazzo and Belkin quoted Dena Luna, a leader in the Minneapolis Public School sector in their article, who stated:

"A lot of times within our education system, black students are expected to conform to a white standard... In our spaces, you don't have to shed one ounce of yourself because everything about our space is rooted in blackness."

Advocates of the approach believe that the race-specific equity initiatives only work with community support and buy-in. Luckily for those advocates, there has been growing support for segregated race-specific strategies in curriculum, student housing, school clubs, and convocation ceremonies at post secondary institutions — and now at secondary schools as well.

In an article written by Katherine Mangan for The Chronicle of Higher Education, she reported on student reactions to recent rollbacks on diversity, equity, and inclusion initiatives. In describing the value of segregated spaces, also commonly referred to as affinity programs, Mangan wrote:

"A sense of connection, experts say, can be critical to academic success... Affinity groups that allow students to socialize with members of their own race let them 'refuel' in a comfortable setting with classmates who understand the

challenges they're facing, many student leaders and experts believe. They're pushing colleges to provide more resources that meet those students' specific needs, whether it's for culturally sensitive counselors, lounges to kick back in, or help navigating financial-aid forms."

Evanston Township High School had nearly 200 students voluntarily enrolled in classes with students of the same race, taught by a teacher of the same race as them. It may be too early to predict, but it is possible that the trend could continue down from high schools to primary schools until we arrive at race-specific kindergarten. I don't think they will push the movement to maternity wards in hospital, but I've been wrong before; I once naively believed previously marginalized people wouldn't advocate for segregation in schools.

Ostrich strategy to safer spaces

There is an inescapable irony in receiving support for segregation from the descendants of the civil rights activist movement, those who fought to end segregation a mere 60 years ago. It appears the current generation of students believe that segregated spaces make them more comfortable and provide a safer environment.

Randazzo and Belkin quote students in the program who were satisfied with the new options:

"It's a safe space. In AP classes that are mostly white, I feel like if I answer wrong, I am representing all black kids. I stay quiet in those classes."

The school board is also considering segregation by gender as well. I assume the thinking is that if people of colour do better in coloured classes, taught by coloured teachers using coloured curriculum, surely girls could benefit from being in female-only spaces.

Perhaps the problematic white people and men can be moved to a separate space where they cannot cause emotional distress to anyone. I guess they could go one step further and demarcate the spaces clearly as WHITE ONLY or MEN ONLY so as to avoid any accidental interactions in these UNSAFE spaces. If only we could predict how that would turnout or had a history lesson to guide us!

An alternative to regression
Of course, my sarcasm and satire aside, there may actually be a better way to tackle social problems. Disparities do exist, wealth and opportunities are unequally distributed. Social determinants of health have real consequences, and life is often just plain unfair. The presumption however that race can serve as a single cause variable seems simplistic and unsophisticated.

I would argue that our fixation on race is actually a major contributing factor to the entrenched experience of racism, at least as described in our contemporary discourse. In 2023 it appears we have forgotten the advances made when "race" was unmasked as nothing more than an arbitrary construct, devoid of scientific reality. In 2023 it appears we have forgotten the advances made when we successfully argued that race was not deterministic. In 2023 it appears we have forgotten the advances made when a court ruled separate is not equal.

A USA Today op-ed writer posited:
"It was the argument of the old-time segregationists that the various races were too different to get along side by side. The best that could be hoped for was that each could stay in its lane and flourish on its own with minimal contact with the others. That's sounding more and more like the sort of thing we're hearing on college campuses, where each group is told that others can't understand its thinking because of its unique experiences, requiring its own safe space."

Or I could just quote a young preacher who addressed a congregation at Holt Street Baptist Church on December 20th, 1956 (the same day the U.S. Supreme Court ruled that segregation on public buses was unconstitutional) who famously said:

"Separate facilities are inherently unequal, and that old Plessy Doctrine of separate but equal is no longer valid, either sociologically or legally."

Strong voices and unique ideas to reduce divisiveness in diversity discourse

Thinkers like Kwame Anthony Appiah and Sheena Mason offer a refreshing alternative to the divisive discourse that has dominated the DEI narrative for the past several years.

Appiah is a prominent social philosopher on pluralism. His book The Lies That Bind offers a critique of the current diversity paradigm. By his analysis, the problem with the contemporary diversity work is its myopic focus on essentialism.

Sheena Mason has a new book scheduled for release in early 2024, in which she masterfully illustrates the limitations of tethering ourselves to antiquated notions of race. It provides a nonpartisan unifying perspective that exposes the myth of race as the mere host upon which the parasitic nature of racism is dependent. Mason breathes much needed new life into the current and often divisive DEI discourse, by de-politicizing the subject and forthrightly tackling the root of the racism problem — race.

If an achievement gap is the problem we are attempting to address, supplying students with a never-ending stream of limiting beliefs hardly seems like a winning strategy. Maybe the conversation should focus on teaching and learning strategies. Maybe the reforms need to be substantive rather than performative.

Cutting Through the Noise: Is it Fair to Demand a ROI from Your DEIB Activities?

Published by Seeking Veritas on Substack: Oct 24, 2023

"Our world is not divided by race, colour, gender or religion. Our world is divided into wise people and fools. And fools divide themselves by race, colour, gender or religion." – Mohamad Safa, Human Rights Activist & UN Representative

A Reflection on DEIB and Leadership

Diversity, equity, inclusion, and belonging; four words
whose origin was noble and well intentioned, whose
journey has meandered through boom-and-bust cycles,
and whose meaning and objectives are much harder to
define in a social context than in a literal one. This article
aims to cut through the noise and provide some social
commentary on the different vantage points from which
to approach this conversation. I will conclude with a
suggested alternative to DEIB for your consideration.

Decentralizing DEIB

The year 2023 has already seen pushback against what
has become mainstream DEIB training. Several
prominent scholars, many themselves people of colour,
have pointed to the divisive tactics that have become
common place. Politicians have identified it as a wedge
issue that can mobilize their respective parties, and a
whole range of entertainers have made DEIB the
punchline of their comedy.

Many corporations have begun slashing DEIB budgets
and scaling back on hiring dedicated staff to fill these
roles. Some academic institutions like Georgia Tech have
already begun decentralizing DEI departments.

*"President Ángel Cabrera announced a new approach aimed
at delivering on the Institute's diversity and inclusion goals.*

Under the new model, existing programs will be embedded across the Institute's academic and administrative units rather than being run out of a separate, central office."

Georgia Tech's new approach incorporates what many DEIB advocates have always argued, namely that DEIB is an operating principle rather than an activity performed by a singular department. As an operating principle, it has sound business value; its proper incorporation should be expected to demonstrate a ROI from the effective coordination of human assets directed towards specific organizational objectives. In all fairness, your average DEIB advocate would make a less capitalistic argument and would probably argue that as an operating principle, they should be granted higher budgets, more authority and the ability to consequence detractors — think Ibram X Kendi's suggestion that government should create an anti-racism bureaucracy with administrative powers.

The new model at Georgia Tech empowers the various academic, service, and administrative units to take ownership of the need to develop inclusive practices directly into their core business, thereby enabling solutions that are better tailored to the unique challenges and opportunities within each area. Rather than have one centralized department responsible for DEIB across the institution, Georgia Tech will establish a Diversity and

Inclusion Strategic Leadership Team with representation from various administrative and academic units to coordinate the work and monitor the Institute's progress. Their current DEIB department will be permanently closed once the new process is launched and the function is decentralized.

Whether this trend will become the norm rather than the exception is still to be seen, but one predictive measure will be its operational capacity to produce results, minimize liability, and stay within scope, schedule and budget.

Social Domain
According to a Pew Research survey, almost one in five newlyweds under the age of 40 in the United States are married to someone of a different race or ethnicity.

In both Canada and the United States, mixed marriages occur more frequently in metropolitan areas compared to rural areas, and there is a positive correlation between higher educational attainment and increased mixed relationships.

According to a 2021 article by The Vanier Institute of the Family, rates of mixed unions (marriage and common law) have steadily increased in Canada over the past several decades. "Based on differences in country of origin, 16% of all couples are in a mixed union ... Approximately one in eight of these couples (12%) include one partner who was born in Canada, and another 4% of couples include two partners born in different countries outside of Canada." In social settings, we have seen generally greater acceptance of social mixing among various ethnicities. Yet most contemporary mainstream DEIB sessions make everyday interactions sound like a Hobbesian reboot of the war of all against all!

DEIB Gurus Criticized by Scholars

Despite the popularity of self-proclaimed diversity experts like Robin DiAngelo, many scholars who also happen to be people of colour find the anti-racism training currently on offer to be infantilizing and condescending to the people it purports to advocate for. John McWhorter, writing for The Atlantic, points to the absurdity of Robin DiAngelo's contradictory claims that white people don't see their whiteness, yet defend it in a highly organized and systematic way. The book White Fragility is in common circulation at Canadian secondary schools and is often paired with Kendi's book How to be an Anti-Racist, much to the chagrin of moderate scholars across the racial and political spectrum.

"I cannot imagine that any Black readers could willingly submit themselves to DiAngelo's ideas while considering

themselves adults of ordinary self-regard and strength. Few books about race have more openly infantilized Black people than this supposedly authoritative tome."– John McWhorter

A 2023 article titled "The Paradox of Diversity Training" by Connor Friedersdorf highlights that "The Harvard Business Review has been publishing articles that cast doubt on the efficacy of mainstream DEI approaches for years." He quotes from a 2018 summary of studies by Harvard University professor Frank Dobbin and Tel Aviv University professor Alexandra Kalev stating that "Hundreds of studies dating back to the 1930s suggest that anti-bias training does not reduce bias, alter behavior or change the workplace." Connor's article highlights that while diversity training has been around for a long time, they are rarely "subjected to rigorous evaluation, and those that mostly appear to have little or no positive long-term effects."

I do feel a level of sympathy for all those consultants and advisors who have found employment in this era or have made a killing over the last several years; they seem to have become the overnight punching bag of choice for moderates and conservatives. The biggest sting to their reputation actually coming from critics otherwise considered liberal, who find their firebrand style simply a bridge too far.

Hedging Their Bets

After 2020 shareholder capitalism momentarily gave way to stakeholder capitalism and its cousin ESG (short for environmental, social and governance). According to the Fraser Institute stakeholder capitalism posits that "businesses should not purely focus on maximizing returns to owners but rather use the resources of companies to solve social problems, thus maximizing benefits to various 'stakeholders' (i.e. their employees, customers, suppliers, communities and countries). ESG remains a subjective concept used for a wide range of causes from climate policies to 'diversity' initiatives."

Major corporations and academic institutions hedged their bets and jumped headfirst into political and social activism. They were sure they were on the right side of history, missing the obvious fact that only the history of the future could adjudicate about that. Nonetheless, they rode that train for a solid three years before the wheels started to come off.

As social problems globally get drawn into the simplistic diversity discourse, the reductive default arguments have begun to falter under the weight of complexity. Social media works really well for outrage that lasts for only a couple of news cycles. The challenge with real world problems, however, is that they are harder to make pronouncements about and simply move to the next big thing. Unfolding social problems have a way of morphing and changing over time and context, often only increasing in complexity.

As we move into the next phase of this ongoing social debate, corporations and institutions may increasingly seek to decentralize their DEIB infrastructure, develop meaningful performance metrics and demand a reportable return on investment. The pitfalls of responding too quickly to social trends with large infusions of cash and limited accountability are becoming plainly apparent. The days of check box tokenism may actually be coming to an end.

A New Way Forward: Excellence, Opportunity, and Access

As promised, I conclude with a suggested alternate to DEIB for your consideration. The past has undoubtedly been unjust to many and downright abhorrent to millions. But the thing about the past is that it is unchangeable, something we can learn from, and whose mistakes we can strive not to repeat ever again. Mistakes like the belief in a hierarchy of humans based solely on a constructed concept of race that has no basis in science or reality.

One option is to take the advice of anointed gurus like DiAngelo who thinks there is no way to ever turn the corner, or Ibram X Kendi who forthrightly advocates that the best redress to past negative discrimination is current "positive discrimination." I opt to take a different path, one that does not type-cast millions of people into reductive groups. One that does not reduce the individual to a cog in a machine with no agency.

To me, barriers are barriers, and we need to find the best way to bring out the excellence within people, services, and outcomes by making opportunities accessible to as many people as possible. We need to bring more people into the conversation; we need to commit to progress and optimism for the future.

When all else fails, I leave you with this to ponder; let me share my lived experience as a brown man, whose people were colonized by the Portuguese and the British well into the twentieth century:

"I've met geniuses and dullards; empaths and sociopaths; optimists and pessimists; philosophers and bullshitters; I've met people with character and integrity as well as douchebags that rode in on donkeys... but nature did not discriminate, instead she distributed them equally among every race in every place. My lived experience has shown me that excellence and stupidity are equally distributed across humanity; so, you get to choose whether you join the wise people or the fools." – Neil Gonsalves

Generative AI, DEIB, and Our Inability to Get Out of Our Own Way

Published by Seeking Veritas on Substack: Oct 31, 2023

"The hardest thing to learn in life is which bridge to cross and which to burn." – Bertrand Russell

I recently attended a brilliant session on Generative AI and its application within the educational sector. There were a lot of great presentations and engaging topics discussed, but I'm going to focus on two occurrences that may encourage some introspection as we immerse

ourselves in the constantly evolving world of Artificial Intelligence. Both incidents passed almost unnoticed yet registered with me for very personal reasons.

The keynote speaker demonstrated a piece of technology that could give the appearance that a user was maintaining eye contact on a video call even when he wasn't. The demo video showed an actor on a split screen, one labeled reality and the other AI generated. In reality, the actor was looking down at his phone, but the AI overlay made it appear as if he was still engaged on the call. Everyone in the room laughed, and a few jokes were made about how meetings would be less monotonous if we could actually be on our phones.

At another point in the presentation, we were shown a program that would allow users to take a picture of something and have AI describe all the complex elements captured in the image. We chuckled again when we saw examples about how we could read convoluted parking signs, or have homework done by AI analyzing an image and providing a write up.

I think skepticism is baked into the genetics of homo-sapiens; no sooner than we come up with a new technology, we begin to spiral down a rabbit hole of doubt and cynicism. Somehow, we always end up trying to predict the future based on the worst versions of ourselves that we can conjure in our minds eye. Why is that I wonder? Are we truly that resistant to change? No matter how much progress we make, some tropes are permanently etched in our cultural consciousness. Have you ever been able to get through an AI presentation without at least one reference to SkyNet, Cyberdyne or a Judgement Day pitting machines against humanity? I know I haven't! Yet many of us forget that movie came out in 1984, at a time when some of us were still contemplating low price VHS vs. high quality Betamax. That's almost forty years ago. Video seems to have evolved, but not our fear of SkyNet!

Everyone gets a big chuckle at tropes about computers killing us, but something unintentional happens in every one of those rooms that we often miss. Our collective fears start to slowly creep into the space, without anyone necessarily noticing it, and our receptiveness subconsciously gets tainted. We normalize subtle anxieties, and a conscious decoupling of ourselves from the technology we create occurs. For all the wonders of AI, it's fascinating to me that we get stuck on more trivial concerns like cheating or slacking on the job. It may be worth noting that neither cheating nor slacking ever needed the help of technology. People have always been sufficiently motivated to do both in the most creative ways.

To some extent, many of us have a bias that technology makes us lazy or less productive, ironic because every AI presentation actually focuses on the redundancies technology can eliminate and the increased productivity we can realize. So why do we keep getting in our own way? If we set aside our propensity for doubt, our often-contagious pessimism in other people, and our innate ability to crap on everything new, we might realize that the potential of Artificial Intelligence actually rests within each one of us. It is our expertise, our experience and our creativity that is augmented by technology. It allows us to do a little more of what we already want to do, be a little better at what we already need to be better at, and be more efficient with what we already strive to be more efficient at. It doesn't replace us; it enhances our capacity to do more of what we are already passionate about.

Let me illustrate my point by returning to the examples I provided at the beginning of this article. I am an advocate for viewpoint diversity, plurality and inclusivity based on our common humanity. If I put my DEIB hat on and reframe the content I listened to during that presentation utilizing my expertise, experience and knowledge, the jokes fade away and the value come into focus. The eye contact AI overlay could surely be used to hide disengagement, but it could also be used by people like me with visual deficiencies.

I suffered from a genetic eye disease as a child that resulted in me losing 95% vision in my right eye and 55% in my left. I was two weeks away from being blind when I received my first cornea transplant. Today I don't live with the disease, but my vision is less than optimal. Our transition to virtual meetings and presentations is hard on my eyes, especially by midday, so I joke about preferring in person meetings, mostly because I dread the screen share and discussion around some tiny detail on the screen. The eye contact overlay would allow people like me to lean in, squint, and strain without making us feel self-conscious or forcing us to turn off our camera (nowadays viewed as a sign of disengagement itself). It could be a tool of inclusion and access which also preserves our health privacy.

The second scenario was originally viewed as a shortcut for parking or a way to make homework easier. Reframed from an access and inclusion lens, however, it provides the opportunity for a family (perhaps currently on a long wait list for a family doctor) to take a picture of their sick child's throat; the AI perhaps could use the image to scan for white patches or streaks of pus on the tonsils, tiny red spots on the roof of the mouth, or others markers that could be statistically indicative of strep throat. Perhaps if verified for accuracy with a high degree of confidence, the image could trigger an automated call in to the local pharmacy resulting in a prescription for antibiotics. All of that might save that family from having to sit at a walk-in clinic for hours. It may prevent someone from having to book off from work. It could level the playing field for people who do not have a family doctor.

It could even lighten the strain on the health care sector, an objective in keeping with the Province of Ontario's attempt at making it more convenient for people to connect to care closer to home. According to a January 2023 press release from the Office of the Premier, "Allowing pharmacists to prescribe for these common ailments and renew prescriptions makes it easier for Ontarians to receive the care they need, while offering patients additional choices for how they receive health care."

Those are just two examples of Generative AI augmenting my knowledge and experience as a DEIB advocate. I turned two quick jokes and dismissed moments into something that matters to the people seeking access to full social participation. Now if each of us shared how our expertise and experience informed the message from that session, imagine how many lost knowledge opportunities we might recover together!

Section 4 -
CHALLENGES IN THE EDUCATION SYSTEM

Summary

The Canadian education system is often lauded for its inclusivity and diversity, yet beneath the surface lies a complex array of challenges that educators grapple with daily. Professor Neil Gonsalves is a firsthand witness to the struggles faced by both students and faculty in navigating an evolving academic landscape. From the pressures of accommodating increasingly diverse student populations to the growing demand for technology integration, our institutions are at a crossroads. Balancing tradition with innovation, equity with excellence, and accessibility with sustainability requires a reimagining of how education is delivered.

This series of articles delves into the critical issues affecting Canadian education from the unique vantage point of those working within the system. They explore themes such as funding disparities, government policy and decision-making, and dealing with the challenges of preparing graduates for an uncertain future. He also addresses the rise of DEI, cancellation, and conversations about the systemic barriers that hinder equity in education/His personal insights and thoughtful reflections aim to foster a deeper understanding of the complexities within our education system and ignite conversations about meaningful change.

Straight "A" Students: Progress or Red Herring?

Published by Seeking Veritas on Substack: Nov 19, 2024

Exploring the impacts of grade inflation and the commodification of education on social mobility and student success.

Why do you send your kids to school? Other than the obvious legal requirements while they are minors, most people acknowledge that school serves two distinct functions. Formally it is meant to provide the foundational skills necessary for future advanced learning, and informally it serves as an important means of socialization. Post secondary level education by comparison is valued by its related function of creating opportunities for social mobility.

For a select few whose social status puts them among the most affluent, ascriptive characteristics like family of origin will routinely guarantee their progeny social reproduction. But for the vast majority of people intergenerational mobility carries significant importance.

Parents, usually but not always, have an innate desire to see their children succeed and surpass the achievements of previous generations. This typically involves being better educated, more qualified, and more likely to achieve progressive employment that will create opportunities for a better life. For the people without affluence, achieved rather than ascribed characteristics of their children will play a significantly greater role in determining their future opportunities.

Assuming a reasonable level of accuracy in my description above, then the achievement process must reasonably require a level of proficiency and mastery in one's chosen field of study in order to enable opportunities for social mobility. Educational institutions logically should serve as the catalyst for the required skill and knowledge development.

But does the modern education system actually meet this standard?

Inflated Grades

There are growing concerns within academia about grade inflation at both the secondary and post-secondary levels. Oxford Learning defines grade inflation as "a trend that gradually increases average grades over time, often without a corresponding improvement in students' actual academic performance". □

Data from six large school boards representing one-third of Ontario's student population showed the proportion of Grade 9 students with 90-plus averages rose significantly after the COVID pandemic school closures. The Toronto Star reported data that indicated "Grade 12 averages are on a steady slope upwards and the number of kids entering university with a 95+ average has exploded."

The□Canadian University Survey Consortium found that 70 per cent of first-year students reported having an A-minus average or above in high school. Dan Côté, a sociologist from University of Western Ontario points out that in the early 1980s that number was only 40 per cent. -

So, are kids today significantly smarter than students in the 1980s?

The trend towards higher grades would not be a concern if it was truly accompanied by an increase in student proficiency, except studies consistently demonstrate that Canadian students have declining academic performance. Between 2018 and 2022 math and reading literacy levels have dropped 14 points on average, and those drops in proficiency have been a consistent trend for more than a decade.

Dwayne Benjamin, the University of Toronto's vice provost of strategic enrolment management, says grade inflation also creates challenges for incoming students. "They may have an exaggerated sense of their own preparedness... Grades are information. Grade inflation distorts the information and degrades the quality of the information".

Students regularly harangue teachers and professors for higher grades based on their efforts rather than their output. Students have become so accustomed to negotiating for higher grades that they are often offended at faculty who won't entertain the bargaining.

Jean Twenge, a San Diego State University professor, theorized in her book 'Generation Me' that overconfidence prevents young people from learning how to deal with failure. The inflated grades give students the false impression that they are more gifted than they actually are, causing students to struggle after high school.

Fortunately for struggling students and much to the chagrin of any educator still committed to teaching and learning, post-secondary institutions are just as guilty of inflating grades as high schools.

A Forbes article shared a report that indicated 44% of educators surveyed say that students today often ask for better grades than they've earned. Four out of five educators say they've given into these demands because parents and students have become increasingly assertive, and "many school leaders and educators have decided that it's easier to appease them than to fight them". They attribute this to education leaders and advocates becoming uncomfortable with traditional notions of rigor or grading.

The other reason students and parents have begun to sound more like customers can be attributed to the commodification of education writ large.

McDonaldization of Education

The commodification of education refers to the transformation of education into a marketable commodity resulting in the commercialization of educational institutions. It shifts education from a public good to a private commodity that can be purchased. Professor Basilio G. Monteiro at St. John's University, New York argues that the corporatization of educational institutions has become the norm and most educational institutions being tuition-dependent, operate with perennial anxiety about generating "a diverse stream of revenue." The accelerated decrease of government funding has resulted in revenue generation being placed at the centre of every deliberation and decision in managing academics institutions.

The economics of education have changed the dynamics within educational institutions. Post-secondary institutions adopted a client-centric approach to students, assigning a high value to perceived student satisfaction and customer retention. Treating students like customers rather than learners has predictably resulted in students acting like customers. Bad grades make for unhappy customers, unhappy customers leave bad reviews and tend to shop elsewhere for their products, and that has an adverse impact on the bottom line. This often creates the unfortunate environment within which worrying about customer retention takes priority over the foundational principle of education as a social good.

The biggest losers in this dynamic are actually the students themselves. A failure to achieve foundation learning skills and subject mastery will have a lasting impact on their career trajectory, as well as their problem solving and critical thinking abilities, not to mention their social development and capacity for resilience in the future.

If you want a standardized product, that is probably bad for your long-term health, requires limited effort on your part, and is delivered with little regard to your wellbeing, may I suggest visiting your local McDonalds.

ECON 101
In Canada, during the 1960s, most people finished high school, entered the workforce and began families. Only a small number of people, approximately 10% entered university, by 2021 that number grew significantly to approximately 66 per cent of Canadians aged 25–34 having a post-secondary education. Let's just focus on some basic economics here. Pricing broadly, and wage rates generally, are established by the laws of supply and demand. (Greater the demand, lower the supply, higher the price). Within the labour market the price of labour is based on the availability of the resource. The fewer

skilled and educated workers available to fill the
required position, the greater the demand, the higher the
wage rate. Conversely, increasing the number of
credentialed people looking to enter the labour market
will lead to an inflation in the qualification requirements
for jobs and a corresponding compression of the wage
rate, along with increased reliance on precarious labour.

The Pew Research Center estimates that young adults
today are significantly better educated than previous
generations and yet have less financial stability. - So
much for social mobility and a better quality of life.
Reset

Regardless of whether you are a parent, or a student here
are a couple of things worth considering:

- If everyone gets an "A" it renders the grade
meaningless. It suggests limited opportunity for
growth and learning. It logically means that you are
average because that is how math works! You cannot
have the same grade as just about everyone else and
simultaneously claim to be smarter than everyone
else.
- Receiving feedback that highlights where you can
improve is the point of a meaningful education. If
you treat every grade, you don't like as automatic
grounds for a complaint or appeal, you remove the

opportunity to learn from failure. I'm not sure when we made failure a bad word, but it surely isn't helping young people. Learning from failures is an integral part of mastery. We used to call it failing forward, and it referred to the capacity to learn, grow, and develop the areas where we had skill, knowledge, or experience gaps.

- Equality of outcome is a utopian fantasy. We can't all be in the 1%. Again, because that is not how math works! Our society needs doctors, lawyers, and engineers but we also need tradespeople, public works, and hospitality staff. Our focus should be on dignity of labour and equality of opportunity for all, but equally important is recognizing the pragmatic reality that a functioning society requires people to fill a myriad of roles - and not all of them require a post-secondary education.

I'd like to leave you with two quotes from Randy Pausch, author of the book 'The Last Lecture'. They may actually help more than the grades people feel the need to demand.

"Experience is what you get when you didn't get what you wanted. And experience is often the most valuable thing you have to offer."

"When you're screwing up and nobody says anything to you anymore, that means they've given up on you."

Dear College President, Pay Attention School is in Session

Published by Seeking Veritas on Substack: Jun 12, 2023

The 2017 student protest at Evergreen State College serves as an excellent case study for colleges and universities who lose sight of their core function of education, in favour of virtue signalling and staying trendy. Located in Seattle, Washington, Evergreen State College is a small public college known for its liberal disposition. A series of events between 2011 and 2017 put faculty, administration, and students on a collision course.

In 2011, the college changed its mission statement to highlight its commitment to diversity and social justice. Over the next several years, the college president George Bridges, along with several administrators and faculty, committed their attention to a campus wide equity agenda. The president even started signing all his memos and communications with the phrase, "education-solidarity-inclusion."

At the 2015 campus call to action forum, the agenda specifically focused on the experiences of racialized faculty and students. White faculty made public statements acknowledging and affirming the following statements:

- *All white people benefit from racism.*
- *To not act against racism, is to support racism.*
- *Even though student experience is a better guide, professors are considered more credible — positionality must be constantly addressed.*

By 2016, the equity council had drafted a new equity policy. A meeting was called to discuss it; the policy was not sent out to faculty until a few minutes before the meeting. At the meeting, however, the new policy was being celebrated, not discussed. A member of the equity council stated unequivocally:

"We are going to do it — don't get it twisted. We invite you join us but if you want to be an obstructionist then you can go work alone."

The faculty at the meeting were told that anyone who opposes the policy is racist. The equity council representatives provided campus wide presentations, highlighting the importance of the student voice and their need to take control of the policies that impact them. The students were energized and engaged, and at a student council meeting shortly thereafter, students called on each other to develop new strategies to address the systemic racism that they were experiencing. Three suggestions were offered:

1. Political organization.
2. Non-traditional more violent direct action.
3. Prayer.

Since the 1970s, staff, faculty and later students participated in a social awareness exercise called Day of Absence. Participants of colour spent one day off campus in order to make their absence and their vital role in campus life felt. In 2017, the event organizers made one significant change. Instead of people of colour opting not to come to campus, that year all white students and staff were asked to stay away from campus.

The Day of Absence went by without significant incident. However, about a month later, Professor Bret Weinstein, a biology professor who considers himself to be fairly progressive, found himself on the pointy end of the social justice activism spear. He had objected to the idea of asking one group based on the colour of their skin to go away from campus. He suggested there was a categorical difference between choosing to opt out of something and being told to go away. He communicated those thoughts to other faculty via email.

On May 23, 2017, a group of angry students cornered Professor Weinstein in a hallway in protest and berated him for the email. They called him a "piece of shit" and demanded that he resign, claiming his email dissent regarding the Day of Absence was racist and harmful to students. Professor Weinstein attempted to communicate with the students, but they responded that they "are not speaking on terms of white privilege." The students, echoing comments made by faculty a couple years previously, shouted that they didn't need to learn about racism because their lived experience gave them all the knowledge they required.

Students concerned about Weinstein's safety called the police. However, the protesting students physically prevented the campus police from reaching him. As the situation began escalating, students claiming to be fearful for their lives due to systemic racism marched to President George Bridges office to confront him. The president attempted to speak to them, but the group yelled at him:

"Fuck you George, we don't want to hear a goddamn thing you have to say so shut the fuck up."

The president complied and organized a meeting with other administrators and the protestors. At the meeting, the protestors let administrators know that "their white silence was violence." Students expressed their frustration that faculty were allowed to disagree with the new equity policy. They were even more alarmed that faculty were allowed to email their dissent. President Bridges agreed faculty who dissent were a problem. He stated that he understood that faculty needed to be brought in for training on equity and if they still didn't get onboard, they needed to be sanctioned. He asked the students protestors to hold him accountable to that pledge. To be clear, he was pledging to sanction faculty dissent!

While negotiations were in progress, other students
barricaded buildings with furniture preventing faculty
and administrators from leaving. They also prevented
campus police from entering. The escalating action was
now at levels considered criminal, however, the
president directed campus police to stand down and not
take action against the student protesters.

By the next day, President Bridges and senior
administrators met with the student leaders who issued a
list of demands. The students demanded the following
"reparations" for the impact of Professor Bret Weinstein's
email:

Mandatory bias training for faculty.
Refund of the semester tuition.
Permission to not turn in their homework.
Free food for the next quarter.

That night, Professor Naime Lowe, from the media
faculty, emailed everyone on campus congratulating the
students for doing exactly what they had been taught to
do. Earlier in the day she attended campus, even though
she was off for the day to lend her support to the
students. She berated her fellow faculty members, stating
they were complicit. She urged them to support the
students and stated she had stopped coming to faculty
meetings because they were all racists. Bret Weinstein,
the target of the students' derision, received support

from only one faculty member other than his own wife, Heather Heying. She was a faculty member at Evergreen State College for fifteen years.

When all the dust settled, Professor Weinstein and his wife Professor Heying were asked to leave the college because they were not wanted for the fall semester. By September 2017, they both resigned. The campus police chief Stacy Brown, who was helpless to maintain order and safeguard the staff given the president's order to stand down, also resigned. The college president stayed on; he had agreed to many of the protesters demands and announced that he was grateful for the passion and courage of students. None of the student were sanctioned for their involvement in criminal activity, including forcible confinement. President Bridges even hired one of the student leaders of the protest to join his Presidential Equity Advisors.

There are several key takeaways worth exploring:

- For senior leaders in administration: The long-term reputation damage from the protest led to consistent declines in enrolment over the next several years. Failure of leadership exacerbated the problem, and ultimately impacted the bottom line.
- For faculty: Being an educator is about educating, not indoctrinating. When a disproportionate amount of

time is invested in a singular ideology and dissent is stifled, the result is predictable — uninformed activism and self-righteous indignation.

- For students: Getting swept up in mob mentality is fairly common when emotions run high. A lot has been written on the subject that may be worth exploring. Activism is undoubtedly a positive part of a free and democratic society. However, simultaneously failing to respect the basic rights of other individuals in that same free society is hypocritical.

The common thread for all three groups: good intentions, unchecked and unbalanced, can result in unintended negative consequences.

All that being said, if I had to be completely objective, I would have to admit that the students succeeded. Their demands were met; none of them were sanctioned; their leader got a job with the college as an equity advisor; the police chief resigned; and the faculty member who dared to dissent was forced to resign!

Perhaps the students said it best:

"Didn't you teach us to do shit like this? The institution is here to serve us, that is what we pay for!"

Maybe when we started treating students like customers, we were destined to face the perception that the customer is always right!

Identity Affirming Safe Spaces

Published by Seeking Veritas on Substack: Feb 7, 2024

My writing partner and dear friend wrote this sentence to wrap up his article titled "Black History Month" earlier this week:

"Black people have been historically under-represented and face many more systemic barriers. That is why we recognize Black History Month. It is an opportunity for all of us to learn this history and better understand the struggle Black people in Canada face, even now."

323

Canadian history is replete with examples of human failings and an unwillingness to recognize the common humanity of our fellow citizens. That black people suffered the impact of ignorance and bigotry is not in dispute.

Africville, the small community in Halifax, Nova Scotia, Canada is a reminder of the unequal treatment that was common mid-way through the last century. Africville existed from the early 1800s to the 1960s. While the area has since been condemned, the site is now recognized as having historical significance; a memorial and museum now stand where the community once existed. If you are unfamiliar with the story of that community, you should definitely look it up. I think it should be taught in schools so that the egregious errors of the past are not repeated. The intergenerational scars still exist, and no matter what progress occurs, the history will never go away — that's just how history works!

I often write about the shortcomings of many contemporary approaches to remedying historical wrongs and the strategies commonly being employed today in the name of equity. In this article, I'm going to highlight perspectives I don't normally cover so as to platform the counterarguments to my usual content. I also offer the content without editorial comment.

Core Tenets of Anti-Racist Scholarship-Activism.

1. Racism exists today in both traditional and modern forms.
2. All white people benefit from racism regardless of intentions.
3. To not act against racism is to support racism.
4. Racism must be continually identified, analyzed and challenged. No one is ever done.
5. Resistance is a predictable reaction to anti-racist education and must be explicitly and strategically addressed.

While the list above is not exhaustive, it captures some of the most common arguments I've heard. As Ibram X Kendi, author of How to be an Anti-Racist, states:

"The only remedy to racist discrimination is antiracist discrimination. The only remedy to past discrimination is present discrimination. The only remedy to present discrimination is future discrimination."

Kendi is the founder and director of the Center for Antiracist Research at Boston University. He was included in Time's 100 Most Influential People of 2020. He also supports and praises the efforts of Robin DiAngelo, author of White Fragility, for her "unapologetic critique" of white people and her apparent indifference to "the feelings of the white people in the room" when she presents her view that white people should not think that because they marched for civil rights in the 1960s, or served diverse communities, or were progressive adherents of liberalism, that they were exempt from being considered racists. In fact, she argues that if you're a white person in America, you're a racist, and without a lifetime of conscious effort you always will be.

These views are not uniquely American. Canadian post secondary institutions have also heard the tenets of anti-racism and are working hard to create remedies for past injustices while creating spaces for belonging and inclusion. They are doing this by carving out safe spaces exclusively for people who are black so they can recharge from the trauma caused by being around white people who don't admit to carrying their invisible white knapsack.

An associate Professor at Toronto Metropolitan University (TMU) explained that the type of racism black people experience is different than other marginalized groups. A sentiment echoed by several universities who signed a 2021 document titled the Scarborough Charter on Anti-Black Racism. As a direct result of their adoption of the charter, several universities have intentionally created "identity affirming safe spaces" exclusively for black folx. (Folx: a modern variation similar to Womxn or

Latinx meant to emphasize inclusion of all groups of people in a gender-neutral manner.)

For black Folx who need to heal, recharge, and build community in spaces free from people of other races, there are a growing list of options:

1. The University of Toronto (U of T) was the first Canadian institution to have a racially segregated graduation ceremony that currently takes place on campus every year.

2. Other Canadian universities that currently offer segregated, black-only convocations include, McMaster University, Toronto Metropolitan University, Simon Fraser University, and Concordia University. McGill University holds a full convocation ceremony but also has an upscale black-only event at a high-end hotel.

3. Twice a week, the University of Waterloo athletic centre reserves its pool for exclusive use by black people. The program is officially called "Black Folx Swim," a 60-minute black-only pool time. Users can swim lengths, practice diving, or sign-up for a lesson. But they — and all the instructors — must be "Black folx." The Black Folx Swim is the university's only demographic-specific swim time.

5. The University of British Columbia has opened The Black Student Space as an identity-affirming space

available only for black undergraduate and graduate students currently enrolled at the UBC Vancouver campus.

6. Toronto Metropolitan University, formerly Ryerson, has a Black Student Lounge. The space is intended as a shelter from "the harms of institutional racism." In multiple public statements, TMU has referred to itself as a hotbed of colonialist institutional oppression, and the lounge is intended as a place where students can "heal" and "recharge" from said oppression, and "promote black flourishing."

7. The University of Toronto offers a black-only frosh week and orientation activities.

8. York University (Canada's second-largest university) also has a lounge for black students only.

9. Simon Fraser plans to build a black student centre.

By most indicators, it appears the concept of black-only spaces is gaining popularity. In America, there are already options for segregated housing at American universities. That may become an option available to future students who don't want to mix with other races in Canadian post-secondary institutions.

Should We Cancel All Dead White Men?

Published by Seeking Veritas on Substack: Jun 11, 2023

"I sit with Shakespeare, and he winces not. Across the color line I move arm in arm with Balzac and Dumas, where smiling men and welcoming women glide in gilded halls. From out the caves of evening that swing between the strong-limbed earth and the tracery of the stars, I summon Aristotle and Aurelius and what soul I will, and they come all graciously with no scorn nor condescension." – W.E.B. Du Bois, The Souls of Black Folks, 1903

What do we do about all the dead white men in our curriculum? A recent trend in the culture wars ostensibly aims to balance perspectives between those considered to be the founding fathers of most academic subjects with marginalized voices left out of the standard post-secondary curricula. In practical application, the trend has taken the form of boycotting thinkers identified as male and caucasian, especially if they're old or dead! The rationalization for challenging the prominent role of such thinkers is based on the belief that they represent a euro-centric, white and male perspective that ignores the humanity of women and marginalized peoples.

It is indeed counterproductive to offer unreflective reverence to a select group of thinkers and become myopic in our worldview. Dogma about a limited canon of knowledge can only take us so far. And as a matter of fact, contemporary scholarship has contributed in meaningful ways to our academic discourse. We should strive to add those contributions to the plethora of sources from which we develop our understanding on any given subject. But while there is little doubt that the voices, perspectives, and scholarship of marginalized peoples should be included in standard curricula, the practice of subtracting rather than adding to the body of knowledge available to learners is a problematic trend for many reasons.

Let's first address the elephant in the room: many of the thinkers commonly considered the behemoths of academic disciplines were imperfect human beings, and some were downright abhorrent in their disposition when measured against contemporary social values. Therein lies the problem, however; it is a curious strategy to posthumously condemn someone on the basis of a social standard that did not exist in their time. Abiding by a social standard implies a rational choice between competing perspectives, but how does one choose a perspective that is not yet a common social standard? Is it really justified, then, to remove someone from the canon because they didn't measure up to our current standard? Does the fact that they shared their contemporaries' values invalidate their academic work?

Consider this thought experiment to illustrate the point: before you make your next statement, perform your next action, or express your next opinion, evaluate how your thoughts, actions and opinions will be judged a couple of centuries from today. Then act in accordance with what a future society would consider acceptable.

Can you identify the challenge with such a strategy? Consider how you might even answer such a question; logically, you would have to presume to know what social values will remain unchanged, anticipate how future social movements will alter the prevailing social attitudes of that time, and then make a range of assumptions about what a future generation, yet to exist, would find socially acceptable. Ultimately, you would end up stacking assumption over assumption and give priority and preference to your own current values and morals as a guiding principle. So why would people in any other time approach this situation any differently?

Let me be very clear, though; I am not saying that some past attitudes and behaviours aren't morally reprehensible to us in the twenty-first century. I am definitely not saying we should celebrate the atrocities that were inflicted upon millions of humans over history. What I am arguing against is the need to erase or censor every thought, opinion and theory on the basis that its creator was a product of their time and failed to meet the basic standards of decency that we expect in our times.

It goes without saying, thinkers had no way of knowing the prevailing social values of a twenty-first century society. They too would have been dumbfounded by the thought experiment I posed earlier. Arguably, they too might have made assumptions that the world would remain fairly consistent, and their assumptions would have been based on giving their own morals and values priority and preference. Consider that the world has followed strict, arbitrary, and coercive hierarchies for most of known human history; this statement was true well into the twentieth century and in many places within our global community, that statement is still true today.

In order for us to contend with the society we live in, we need to understand the systems that inform and structure it. Regardless of how we perceive previous generations, it is impossible to get away from the reality that much of western morality, political thought, and social structures are based upon the teachings, writings, and canonical theories of the founding fathers, flaws and all.

Were there great thinkers within the population of marginalized people whose voices were muted? Of that I have no doubt. And while we should strive to find these voices and bring them to life, we shouldn't, by the same token, systematically reject the voices of scholars who, despite their influential work, turned out to be on the wrong side of moral history. Life has not always been equal, nor is it universally equal today. The history of the world is such, and in many ways the circumstances of our present (and wishing it wasn't so) does not change it.

But this begs the question: why study dead white men? Lindsay Johns, the Head of Arts and Culture and a fellow at the Hutchins Center for African & African American Research at Harvard University, whose main research interests include the black canon, the intersection of culture and race, and social mobility, argues that decolonizing the white western Eurocentric canon is not a well-informed decision for a number of reasons.

First, the past is unchangeable and needs to be accepted with a critical eye that promotes learning from the numerous practical applications it provides. Second, he argues that despite any character shortcomings, these thinkers' ideas have stood the test of time because they had value and provided meaningful additions to human understanding. In other words, separating the quality of the idea from the person is a useful lesson in objectivity. Third and most saliently, he argues that solely utilizing representation based on skin colour, gender or sexuality is puerile and disingenuous. Ultimately, accepting the thinkers of yesteryear and desiring to include contemporary scholarship does not have to be mutually exclusive; both can simultaneously exist and add value to our learning and understanding.

To argue that people of colour or historically marginalized people are one monolithic group who require only to hear and learn from our own, is both paternalistic and degrading. It fails to appreciate the intellectual diversity we have as humans. It fails to acknowledge our diversity of thought and opinion. And, most critically, it assumes that the colour of our skin or our shared history of subjugations makes us intellectually incapable of objective reason and nuanced discourse.

Now, it begs the question, why would people seek to erase dead white men when they could simply add marginalized voices. Though I can only make an educated guess, it is worth trying to answer this question. The only good reason why we would want to erase dead white men as opposed to simply adding marginalized voices is to escape the inherent complexity of human nature. By showing competing perspectives, we inevitably run into complicated conundrums. We must be extremely critical and show a high degree of academic rigour.

Unfortunately, when we deal with such emotionally loaded topics, it's easy to seek the easy way out. It's easy to pick one side over the other because it feels right, though it isn't right. Rather than unpacking the complexity of ideas, times, and phenomena, we cast blame, we shame, and we lament. In such an endeavour, we wallow in righteous anger, but we never accomplish anything meaningful. We fail to do the very job we were meant to do, which is to educate.

We should approach life from a mindset of abundance, not scarcity. With a commitment to adding, not subtracting, from the vast amount of knowledge available to us. It can only help us reason more effectively, judge more critically and understand more completely.

I identify as a person of colour. I also identify as a husband, a father, an academic, a bibliophile and a dog lover. The intersections of all my identities are unique to me, as they are to millions of others. But many people, myself included, reject the notion that the colour of our skin determines who we should read and what knowledge we should imbibe. We are more than the colour of our skin, more than our gender, and more than our sexuality. We are people capable of hearing thoughts and ideas from others who do not look like us. And we are capable of being critical toward these ideas.

Do Intentions Matter More Than Outcomes?

Published by Seeking Veritas on Substack: Jun 22, 2023

"Sir, it's not you, there is nothing more you can do; we just don't trust each other. We would never be able to get a job if someone recorded us speaking openly."

That was a comment made to me by a student at the end of a class. For two hours I presented multiple perspectives on contemporary issues related to diversity and law enforcement. Every student dutifully nodded along but would not comment, take a position, or express an opinion; I could not get anyone to participate. For an educator, that kind of silence is deafening! Is this the new classroom norm? What does it say about our society when it appears we have accepted the 2023 reboot of McCarthyism?

I teach a college level diversity course to students who aspire to enter the field of law enforcement. Those who are successful in reaching their goals will be called upon to intervene in conflicts, empathize with victims, and recognize that even those who break the law must be treated in accordance with the principles of procedural justice. These aren't simplistic tasks; they require a degree of critical thinking, and a nuanced understanding of human behaviour.

The classroom environment I described earlier is not uncommon. When I first noticed the trend, my initial reaction was to reflect on my own teaching practices. I wondered if after 17+ years in the classroom I was no longer relevant or relatable. Was there something about me that was the prime mover in their silence?

Perhaps my pop culture knowledge required updating — I'm fairly certain it does! But in all fairness, if it is controversial to talk about, let alone teach, the sociological connection between BLM slogans and the 1988 hit rap song "Fuck the Police" by N.W.A. (yes, I know I cannot actually say what that acronym stands for) then I definitely don't want to discuss the Cardi B song 'WAP' and its relation to women's empowerment! I will keep my pension, thank you!

But therein lies the problem. Too many educators actually believe their pension is at risk for merely teaching academically sound albeit controversial content. What is the root of that problem? An overzealous DEI industry? Administrators? Parenting? Educators? As with most things in life, a single cause variable rarely holds the answer. The fact that many post-secondary educators actually believe they will be unfairly treated if they don't fall in line should be concerning enough; it has a chilling effect on discourse and that behaviour is being actively modelled for the students. Is it any wonder the students elect to self censor?

But is that really an accurate assessment? I've had a lot of conversations with faculty, support staff, administrators, and students over the years. What almost all of them consistently have in common are good intentions and a willingness to attempt the latest strategy that may improve the overall condition of the learning experience. To criticize them for failing some of the time, is antithetical to the principle of a learning organization.

The real challenge might be dealing with very conflicting information, a ridiculously wide range of acceptable strategies, and constantly evolving social dynamics. It is no wonder so many people feel like they are spinning their wheels but going nowhere. Yet, there they are trying each new thing and that is deemed worthy of recognition.

We should highlight to students that the real behaviour being modelled is adaptability, perseverance, and resilience. All of which is necessary when someone feels like they are facing an insurmountable challenge. None of this is intended to excuse bad decisions or corrosive practices. None of this justifies the divisiveness of identity politics. We should be advocating for viewpoint diversity and recognition of our common humanity; that extends to those we disagree with.

"It is not the critic who counts; not the man who points out how the strong man stumbles, or where the doer of deeds could have done them better. The credit belongs to the man who is actually in the arena, whose face is marred by dust and sweat and blood; who strives valiantly; who errs, who comes short again and again, because there is no effort without error and shortcoming; but who does actually strive to do the deeds; who knows great enthusiasms, the great devotions; who spends himself in a worthy cause; who at the best knows in the end the triumph of high achievement, and who at the worst, if he fails, at least fails while daring greatly, so that his place shall never be with those cold and

timid souls who neither know victory nor defeat." –
Theodore Roosevelt

Immanuel Kant argued, intentions are more important than outcomes since they can be more easily determined. If an action is done with good intentions, it is more likely to be moral, even if the results turn out to be undesirable or unsustainable. Perhaps we need to be more charitable in our judgement of intentions and more compassionate in our evaluation of the outcomes, which may be outside the control of any individual person. It is worth remembering Stephen Covey's observation: we tend to judge others by their behaviour but judge ourselves by our intentions! We can do better.

Key Takeaways:

1. We should recognize the positive intentions of those we disagree with. It will enable a deeper understanding of their positions and potentially help in the search for middle-ground.
2. Leaders could do more to instill confidence, so self censorship and paranoia does not become the default position.
3. We need to drown out the noise and be clear about the operational definition of diversity, equity and inclusion within the organization. People need to be

clear on the objective in order to work toward a desired outcome.

Is the Government Devaluing Education?
Part 1

Published by Seeking Veritas on Substack: Jul 18, 2023

"You're going to mess up. So instead of trying to be perfect, learn how to be accountable." – Whitney Goodman

Premier Doug Ford's progressive-conservative government in Ontario has been sharply criticized for a lack of commitment to education. According to Karen Littlewood, president of the Ontario Secondary School Teachers' Federation in a Toronto Star op-ed stated,

"This government has made cuts to education by the billions time and time again, instead of investing in Ontario students and the public education system. Since 2018 Ford has been intentionally underfunding and underspending in education." On education, Premier Doug Ford's unpopularity has not been limited to the secondary school system as he also has his share of critics among post-secondary administrators.

In a Toronto Star article, columnist Martin Regg Cohn argued that Ford's cuts to post-secondary education have put Ontario Colleges and Universities in a state of crisis. He stated that "the system has been slowly starved of cash for more than a decade under both Liberals and Progressive Conservatives... Ontario has refused to raise grant levels, dating back to Dalton McGuinty's Liberal government. That freeze was reconfirmed in April 2023; before the freeze came the cut, an unprecedented tuition reduction ordered by the government in 2019 — entirely at the expense of colleges and universities." Given the fiscal constraints, college and university presidents have been challenged to keep their respective institutions financially viable in the midst of a perfect storm of rising inflation, freezing grants and forced tuition cuts.

If the direct impact to the educational sector is alarming, then those concerns have been amplified recently by the Ford government's recent announcements that seem to devalue post-secondary education in general. In early March, the government announced that they will allow students, starting in Grade 11, to transition to full-time apprenticeship programs while still earning a high school diploma. The move was intended to address the labour shortages given the province's stated intention to build 1.5 million new homes by 2031.

While the impact of such a policy is still being hotly debated, the government followed it with a second announcement less than eight weeks later, this one impacting the policing labour shortage. Premier Doug Ford said at a news conference at the Ontario Police College, joined by Solicitor General Michael Kerzner and Toronto Police Chief Myron Demkiw, that the government would boost lagging police recruitment by eliminating a post-secondary education requirement to be hired as an officer; and the province would also cover 100% of the costs for Basic Constable Training at the Ontario Police College. The three-month program currently costs $15,450. New police officers are required to complete it within six months of being hired. This comes after 2018 reforms to boost recruitment by relaxing the fitness standards for new policing applicants.

Both the March and April announcements may reasonably be interpreted as a direct rebuke of the importance of post-secondary education to the labour market. Back in March, when the first announcement was released, I commented in support of it on a LinkedIn post. I suggested that there is broader social benefit from an active pathway to employment directly out of high school, and that the trades are a perfect starting point. I boldly asserted what we should probably go down the list of occupations and truly audit which fields have a bona fide workplace need for post-secondary education. Within a few minutes of my post becoming public, a person with significant experience in the college system who I have a great deal of respect for contacted me and wanted to discuss my opinion. Given the premium I always place on open discourse, I gladly accepted the invitation.

The person made the case that the government's Skilled Trades announcement rolled back decades of advocacy intended to professionalize the industry. His strongest argument was that the government did not have a clear plan to ensure that those students entering apprenticeship programs prior to completing high school would actually graduate with a secondary school diploma. This may not seem like a significant problem until one considers the 37% attrition rate in the sector. Some of that turnover is positive — promotions, business ventures, etc. — but a lot of it is tied to injuries caused by stress on the body, pressure related to the seasonal nature of work, and social stigma on the quality of the occupation. My trusted interlocutor argued that many of those people would find themselves ill-prepared to transition to other careers in the economy. After all, their highest level of completed education would render them generally unemployable in the broader labour market.

The policing announcement can be seen as equally problematic to post-secondary institutions. Almost all 24 Ontario public colleges, and some private career colleges, offer some version of a Police Foundations or law enforcement-based program targeting aspiring police constables. Notwithstanding recent system wide dips in domestic enrolment, these programs have generally enjoyed the benefit of being both largely popular and relatively low cost to operate. However, they do not attract a large number of international students generally, and this could be a real problem should the announcement have an adverse impact of new applications.

So how did we get here? In Canada, during the 1960s, most people finished high school, entered the workforce and began families. Only a small number of people, approximately 10%, entered university. According to a 2017 article by Steve Paiken of tvo.org titled "Ontario's colleges have come a long way in 50 years", an old wartime factory in Scarborough would be leased out by the federal government allowing the province's first community college to open its doors. Centennial College would become the site of new options for technical and practical education for 500 Ontarians not headed to university.

The Ontario college system of the sixties was intended to be an alternative to university, a more vocationally focused endeavour, directly connected to local economies and the labour market. While universities have been around for hundreds of years, their primary focus and mission was never really about employment, at least not for the masses. Highly specialized university programs that led to professional degrees, medicine, law and engineering for instance directly contributed to the labour force. However, the number of jobs in these fields, when compared to the total number of jobs in the economy, would be statistically insignificant. College was meant to bridge the knowledge gap for blue-collar jobs such as the skilled trades and office administrators; and in so doing, prepare the workforce of tomorrow.

As greater numbers of students entered post-secondary institutions, looking to upskill and upgrade their lives, the dynamics started to shift. They all sought that golden ticket to upward social mobility. They heard the arguments; and they saw the success of all those privileged people who received an education and secured well paying jobs, who lived in larger homes and drove newer cars. It was the Canadian dream, the immigrant dream for all those arriving to call Canada home. It was the promise of a better life, and everyday Canadians were ready to take the plunge. By their estimation, the opportunity cost for delaying entry to the workforce would be minimal given they expected a significant return on their time and tuition money. The only kink in the plan might have been that everyone else had the same plan.

So, is our current situation a reflection of a government hedging its bet on labour over education, hoping the interconnectedness to the two fields can be minimized if we can increase economic productivity? Is the government gambling with the education and skill development of the future labour force? Or is this a market correction that was inevitable given the commodification of education and the rampant credential inflation? Compounded by the erosion of academic rigour compromised in favour of retention; a client-centric approach to students; an obsession with student satisfaction survey results; and more broadly, the diminishing marginal utility of a post-secondary education. Is the government devaluing education? Or have we all played a participatory role?

(This was the first in a three-article series exploring the interconnectedness of the government labour policy and higher education.)

Is the Government Devaluing Education? Part 2

Published by Seeking Veritas on Substack: Jul 18, 2023

"If the idea of having to change ourselves makes us uncomfortable, we can remain as we are. We can choose rest over labour, entertainment over education, delusion over truth, and doubt over confidence. The choices are ours to make, but while we curse the effect, we continue to nourish the cause." –
Jim Rohn

Anti-intellectual — that is how some of the more pointed critics of Ontario Premier Doug Ford have characterized his government's recent announcements. In the last eight weeks, the Premier's office has sought to make significant changes to apprenticeship access for the skilled trades, and to the educational entrance requirements for new police applicants. Both these announcements can be judged fairly as anti-intellectual, given they disregard and reverse decades long progress, advocacy, and consultation between educators and industry intended to benefit workers over their life course. Some see these new initiatives as band-aids on bullet holes, intended for short term political expediency while ignoring the downstream impacts of such choices. If all of that sounds like ivory tower hyperbole, then let's explore the issue and dig a little deeper.

The skilled trades apprenticeship announcement purports to address a significant labour shortage in the trades, one that hamstrings the province's capacity to build new homes at a pace that could influence our current affordable housing crisis. It posits a range of advantages, from youth employment to economic growth based on the newly found earning potential of new trade workers. According to Labour minister Monte McNaughton, one in five job openings in Ontario will be in the skilled trades by 2026. So far, so good; no one seriously disputes that there is a housing crisis, fewer still argue in favour of underemployment, and pretty much everyone agrees that if we don't do something drastic, this current generation will definitely have diminished purchasing power compared to previous generations.

The messaging seems to imply that high school students are ready to enter the workforce, and the apprenticeship route allows them to do so while by-passing post secondary requirements. But are they ready? The government still recognizes the need to fund proper training and development, they just apparently have decided to shut Ontario colleges out. An announcement by the government on March 21, 2023, made explicit their commitment to invest $224 million to build and upgrade private training centres to prepare workers for in-demand careers like electricians, welders and mechanics. The irony is that colleges already have the infrastructure to deliver such training. As a collective, the provinces' twenty-four colleges have ideal geographical dispersement that services the needs of communities across this province. Therefore, it seems to make little sense why the government would explicitly exclude Ontario colleges from the funding.

I spoke with Edward Logan, a faculty member at Durham College who teaches in the skilled trades, to get a first-hand perspective on the issue. He advised me that one of the most popular programs at Durham College is the Trades Fundamentals program, a one-year program taught in one of the college's technology-enabled learning classrooms. The program helps students identify where in the trades they would like to specialize, giving them access to knowledge, skills and abilities related to several trades including carpentry, electrical, plumbing, HVAC and welding. It also exposes them to areas they may not have realized were essential components, such as trades related mathematics and solving trades related applications of ratio and proportion. Clarity and purpose in education are essential to long-term success for students, and the time it takes them at college arguably has many long-term benefits to their future careers.

On the subject of long-term career benefits, the policing announcement is equally troubling. On balance, the proposed changes to Ontario policing recruitment are not all bad. I personally see value in the elimination of the $15,450 tuition fees at the Ontario Police College in Aylmer, Ontario. New constables should not have to pay for the in-service training once hired. Almost every other occupation requires baseline qualifications prior to being hired, but on-the-job training should be the responsibility of the organization that benefits from your labour and productivity. On the other hand, the elimination of the requirement for a post secondary education prior to application ignores research and previous recommendations from the police themselves. It serves as a short-term solution to a recruitment challenge, with significant long-term social implications — potentially detrimental to community safety, public trust and the mental health of future police officers.

A report from the Ontario Association of Police Services Boards that was previously submitted to the province indicated that two-thirds of the 107 boards around the province agreed "post-secondary education ... should be a prerequisite to becoming a police officer." Research shows that, overall, college-educated officers generate fewer citizen complaints; they are also less likely to use force inappropriately. Among front line officers who have the most public interactions, having a post secondary education significantly increases commitment to community policing, promoting a proactive disposition towards working with community members to resolve issues and prevent problems rather than only reacting to calls for service.

As a general rule of thumb, post secondary education increases the capacity for empathy, critical thinking, acting ethically, and being receptive to diverse community demographics. One would assume a global perspective and understanding of various cultures, traditions and norms would be essential given the federal government's immigration targets over the next three years. Education was commonly thought to be the best antidote to ignorance and a vital ingredient of self-awareness.

In my previous article I speculated whether the evidence supported the assertion that the government was playing fast and loose with the labour force of the future. I wondered whether this was a case of them hedging their bets on labour over education to garner public favour and secure future votes. Regardless of whether that is true, there is a significantly more pressing question I think we should contemplate. Namely, where is the public defence of education? Where is the social outrage from all the people who have diligently sent their children to post-secondary institutions? Or the outrage from all the people who have gone back to school to up-skill and upgrade their knowledge? If education is a social good, generating social value, making the world a more informed place, where are community advocates protesting anti-intellectualism?

In the last article in this series, I will explore the participatory role that educators and administrators may have played in possibly eroding public trust. Have we turned a social good into a widget that operates wholly within a capitalist paradigm? For better or worse I love being an educator; but I also believe that it is incumbent on all of us to be objective, to be critical, and to defend or reform this thing that we love. If we are not honest with ourselves, with our colleagues, and with our administrators, then surely, we will be at the mercy of the invisible levers of the market economy. It may be time to ask ourselves whether we are still providing a social good; or have we all accepted that we sell a commodity whose value is subject to the whims of the consumer and the prerogative of our almighty P&L sheets!

(This was the second in a three-article series exploring the interconnectedness of government labour policy initiatives and higher education.)

Is the Government Devaluing Education?
Part 3

Published by Seeking Veritas on Substack: Jul 18, 2023

"Love your enemies, for they tell you your faults"
– Benjamin Franklin

For better or worse, I love being an educator, even when it does not love me back. I believe that it is incumbent on all of us to be objective, to be critical, and to defend or reform this thing that we love. I stand by this notion even as stifling dissent has been normalized and groupthink across most educational institutions is all too familiar. I spoke with several post secondary educators from colleges and universities across the GTA, and none of them wished to be named, quoted or otherwise identified. One even offered me advice as old as time; they thought I should really reconsider this piece and just go along to get along. But, if we are not honest with ourselves, with our colleagues, and with our administrators, then surely, we will be at the mercy of the invisible levers of the market economy, and she is a cruel mistress.

In this last article of the series, I'm exploring the participatory role that educators and administrators may have played in possibly eroding public confidence. We should contemplate the fact that when Premier Ford made his announcements about skilled trades and then policing, there was no public defence of education, nor any social outrage at its devaluing. If education is a social good, generating social value, making the world a more informed place, where were community advocates protesting anti-intellectualism? All of that was conspicuously absent.

When Premier Ford introduced a new funding formula for Ontario Colleges tied to performance and labour market vectors, he put post-secondary institutions on a collision course with the harsh survivalism of the free market. As colleges and universities tap-danced past declining domestic enrolment, and dealt with an unprecedented post-pandemic dystopia, customer satisfaction and retention quickly became a higher priority. Prevailing attitudes turned students into customers. Students who were always stakeholders, were now being treated like shareholders.

Colleges and universities shored up their revenue shortfalls by boosting high value international assets. Those assets are international students whose tuition is not subsidized and is approximately three to four times higher than domestic fees. You just need to watch the Fifth Estate investigative story to see how that turned out. Albeit the piece, while generally well done, failed to highlight the government's participatory role in promoting, profiting, and encouraging the practices that the documentary seemed to lay squarely at the feet of all the colleges, as if they all operated in unison. The conditions and challenges faced by international students are outside the scope of this article, but for our purposes, let's recognize that history has repeatedly demonstrated the folly of treating humans like widgets in an economic process.

Let's just focus on some basic economics here. Pricing broadly, and wage rates generally, are established by the laws of supply and demand. (Greater the demand, lower the supply, higher the price.) Within the labour market, the price of labour is based on the availability of the resource. The fewer skilled and educated workers available to fill the required position, the greater the demand, the higher the wage rate. Competition for jobs that did not require specialized education had generally been determined by factors such as reliable local transportation, access to affordable housing, and a relatively level playing field among similar applicants. Jobs at one point were more appropriately linked to the credentials that employers demanded.

By the time we entered the twenty-first century, there was significant scope creep in the original mandate for vocationally focused Ontario colleges. Many of the new programs and courses were neither vocationally driven nor particularly practical as originally envisioned. In fact, college and universities were competing for students and it did not take long before the mission, purpose and offering at these two types of institutions began to merge, meld and sometimes become indistinguishable. Articulation agreements between colleges and universities became a fairly common practice, a two-year college diploma could now get you into third year university, with some minor conditions. Four years later, a person could boast having a college diploma and a university degree.

The economics of education changed the dynamics within educational institutions. Students, as consumers, demanded ease-of-use from their products. They clearly signalled expectations to receive the certificate they perceived they had already purchased, regardless of their performance. With vocal social media support, social justice activists began pedalling a new brand of constant campus marginalization; even parents seemed more invested in their children's happiness than the mastery of the very subjects they were paying to learn. Through all of this, or perhaps because of it, teachers and professors quickly became impediments, holdouts from a bygone era.

To meet the demands of the labour market — a priority made clear by the government's intended performance-based funding model for post-secondary institutions — the institutions bent over backward to keep 'bums in seats' and supply the economy with qualified workers. The public became convinced that everyone was entitled to an education, and a credential. Employers naturally got on board; a bloated labour supply depresses the wage rate and reduces the need for perks and enticement. Education as a social good was increasingly seen as antiquated. Economic value was the benchmark, and expansion of market share became a symbol of growth. Micro-credentials were brought to market so that just-in-time education was an option for those who could not commit to a diploma or degree. Those students would just become longer term prospects in the sales pipeline; give them a few months and someone would upsell them to a diploma option.

Faculty meetings at many institutions moved away from discussing teaching and learning and shifted towards sales and marketing. Subject matter experts on a variety of academic disciplines would marshal their creative energy towards planning call campaigns and fun recruitment activities, developing marketing events complete with swag and incentives for those impulse buyers. The most common academic content discussions remaining were about developing strategies to minimize course failures, ensuring assessments meet the students where they are at rather than where they ought to be academically, and contending with unprecedented student absences. One faculty member at a GTA college mentioned they routinely have less than 10% of their registered students show up to class regularly, yet feel pressured to ensure that everyone passes the course. Another part-time faculty member, who has been teaching for the better part of the last decade, was adamant that offering criticism would be career suicide.

By focusing on the instrumental reason for obtaining a post-secondary credential rather than the social, emotional and intellectual value the journey offers its participants, post-secondary institutions shifted away from subject mastery, critical thinking, and civic engagement. They shifted away from being a social good. They opted instead to focus on student satisfaction metrics to structure their business. Fear of litigation and human rights complaints now drive decision-making. Fear of revenue shortfalls has informally yet pervasively led to an erosion of academic rigour, compromised in favour of bolstering retention. Utilizing a client-centric approach to students, combined with an unrelenting obsession with student satisfaction survey results, has arguably resulted in the diminishing marginal utility of a post-secondary education.

Employers hiring for unskilled jobs that did not require specialized education, now had a much larger pool to select from. With an abundance of college diplomas and university degrees in circulation, a predictable amount of credential inflation occurred. A job that once went to a high school graduate now required a college diploma, the job that once required a college diploma now required a university degree, and so on. To add another absurd twist, as people started to meet the new standard, a never-ending cycle emerged; everyone embraced continuous learning with the net result being that the same groups of people were still only qualified for the same jobs as before, only this time they were all encumbered with student debt.

Since qualified labour was no longer a scarce resource, recruitment perks would no longer be necessary to entice workers to join a company. The writing would be on the wall for benefits, sick time, vacation time, permanent full-time jobs, pensions, and rewards for tenure.

Welcome to the gig economy, where you get the freedom to work when you want, for as long as you want and wherever you want, because the old economic business model is now dead. You are a special entrepreneur, whose next gig is only a smart phone app away, only it comes at the cost of stability and security. Turns out we might have been better served by introducing an Economics 101 course in high school.

So, is the government devaluing education? Or have we all played a participatory role? In my previous article I speculated on whether the evidence supported the assertion that the government was playing fast and loose with the labour force of the future, or whether Premier Ford's recent announcements were simply signals that it was time for a necessary market correction within post-secondary education. It appears the government's focus on performance had the intended outcome on the culture within academia. In their earnest attempt to tear down the ivory towers, they may just have torn down more than a few of the load bearing walls in the process.

The commodification of education, rampant credential inflation, and a focus on student satisfaction over subject mastery may all have had a detrimental impact on public perception of value. The recent government announcements do seem to diminish the importance of post-secondary education, yet post-secondary end users, the customers and their families aren't outraged. Take away social and political commentary from those associated with academia, and who is left standing with post-secondary defending the social good they produce?

Perhaps it is time to ask if it is just the government that is devaluing education, or have we all played a participatory role in knocking down the tent poles?!

(This was the third in a three-article series exploring the interconnectedness of government labour policy initiatives and higher education.)

Good Governance or Good Press

Published by Seeking Veritas on Substack: Sep 27, 2023

"Darkness cannot drive out darkness; only light can do that.
Hate cannot drive out hate; only love can do that."
– Rev. Martin Luther King Jr.

In 2020, the murder of George Floyd sparked a social movement that accelerated and went viral as quickly as a global pandemic. Boston University, faced with demands from black students and activists to address racial problems on campus, responded by betting that good press was better than good governance.

Intractable Racial Problems

Boston University unveiled the Center for Antiracist Research, which would be headed by a celebrity with no management experience: Ibram X Kendi. While his scholarship is routinely criticized and challenged within academia for its lack of academic rigour, he was highly efficient at raising funds and attracting corporate sponsors, most of whom were highly invested in improving their own diversity credit score. The money poured in, and the Centre received approximately $43-$55 million dollars, the majority of which came in year one; arguably enough to make a significant difference to what Kendi described as "intractable racial problems of our time."

In such tumultuous times, simple messaging travels more efficiently through the frustrated masses, and Kendi offered the right mix of simplicity and pseudo-profundity. He argued that there's no such thing as racial neutrality, and there is no middle ground on race — everyone is either racist or actively antiracist. He believes all disparities in outcomes and achievements of racialized people are a result of racism and discrimination. His anti-racist philosophy was adopted by corporations, educational institutions, and legislators at a dizzying pace.

The Changing Social Tides

The problem with fads and trends that have meteoric growth, however, is that they fall out of favour almost as quickly, and usually leave a swath of well-meaning early adopters in their destructive wake. The first couple of years went really well for the antiracist advocates: DEI departments grew, budgets expanded, and new policies were written and adopted with little consultation and almost no room for dissent. Those years emboldened practitioners and made consultants king, but below the surface, significant problems were becoming apparent. Intellectuals from within racialized groups, including many prominent black scholars, criticized the divisiveness and regressive approach that had become the flavour de jour. The public was quickly tiring of all the blaming and shaming, political tides began shifting and the lawsuits began emerging.

By 2023, three years after its launch, the lack of management experience caught up with Kendi and the Centre for Antiracist Research. Most of their projects were cancelled, little or no research was produced, and most of the staff at the Centre were laid off. Complaints about unethical management of donations were raised, and reports indicated a toxic work environment with high turnover. The Center even tried to manage the demands by hiring an executive director to deal with the day-to-day operations; but the person left the role within less than a year and a half. The situation became so bad that Boston University launched an inquiry into the running of the Centre and the allegations of mismanagement and toxicity.

The Commercialization of DEI

As a result, staff lost their jobs, millions of dollars collected were never properly utilized, and new academic degrees that were proposed never came to fruition. But not all was lost. Kendi's book How to become an Antiracist became a best seller. It allowed for successful spinoffs such as Antiracist Baby, geared for young children, and How to Be a Young Antiracist, targeting tweens and teenagers. Not to miss any opportunity, he also created a guide for parents, aptly named How to Raise an Antiracist. Collaborations with various companies have further yielded anti-racist merchandise and apparel.

His fame has allowed him to diversify his portfolio. He now broadcasts his own Be Antiracist podcast, appears on television as an expert talking head, has his own production company named Maroon Visions, and is also the star of a new exclusive show on ESPN+ called Skin in the Game with Dr. Ibram X. Kendi, purportedly taking on racism in the sports world. All of this over and above the undergraduate course he teaches at Boston University on antiracism and the $20,000 per hour speaking fees for virtual presentations. I suppose a diversified portfolio is really important for a social justice advocate who owns multiple properties in Boston and a vacation residence in Martha's Vineyard.

Doubling Down

"Nothing in all the world is more dangerous than sincere ignorance and conscientious stupidity." – Rev. Martin Luther King Jr.

None of this should come as a surprise: a multimillion-dollar Centre left in the hands of a person with no management experience, new-found celebrity status, unrealistic expectations infused with millions of dollars, and public adoration. What could go wrong?

While Boston University conducts its inquiry on the management of the Centre, they have continued to express support for Kendi, who remains Director. He even has a plan that should make up for all the other failed projects. With the clarity of knowing all his critics are merely trying to "settle old scores," as he explained in an interview, he is going to forge ahead by creating a first of its kind fellowship program for antiracist intellectuals, a nine-month residency program which will include participation in public events while conducting their own research. At this point, it is hard to tell if that's good governance or good press, but the organizational priorities will surely impact its outcome.

Section 5 -
OPINION EDITORIALS IN
NEWSPAPERS

Summary

Opinion editorials, or op-eds, stand as a cornerstone of public discourse, offering readers a platform where diverse viewpoints converge and provoke thought. These pieces, go beyond reporting facts to embrace advocacy, reflection, and critique of the 'common man'. They are a window into the minds of individuals who dare to engage with the pressing issues of our time, from politics and economics to social justice and culture. Through their persuasive narratives, op-eds invite readers to reconsider their mainstream-held beliefs, challenge the status quo, and engage in constructive dialogue about the world we share.

Provincial Move "Ignores Decades of Research and Previous Recommendations"

Published by Metroland Media Group - Durham Region:
May 9, 2023

Anti-intellectual is how some of the more pointed critics of Premier Doug Ford have characterized his government's recent announcements. Ford said at an April 25 news conference at the Ontario Police College (OPC) that the government would boost lagging police recruitment by eliminating a post-secondary education requirement to be hired as an officer and the province would also cover 100 per cent of the costs for basic constable training at the OPC. This after 2018 reforms to boost recruitment by relaxing the fitness standards for new policing applicants.

The announcement regarding the police may be judged fairly as anti-intellectual, given it disregards and reverses decades-long progress, advocacy and consultation between educators and the industry intended to benefit workers over their life course. Some see these new initiatives as Band-Aids on bullet holes, intended for short-term political expediency while ignoring the downstream impacts of such choices. If all that sounds like ivory tower hyperbole, let's unpack the issue a little further.

There is a reasonable argument to be made for the elimination of the $15,450 tuition fees at the OPC. New constables should not have to pay for in-service training once hired. Most other occupations require baseline qualifications prior to being hired, but on-the-job training should generally be the responsibility of the organization that benefits from your labour and productivity. On the other hand, eliminating the requirement for a post-secondary education before application ignores decades of research and previous recommendations from the police themselves. It offers a short-term solution to a recruitment challenge with significant long-term social implications, which are potentially detrimental to community safety, public trust and the mental health of future police officers.

A report from the Ontario Association of Police Services Board, previously submitted to the province, indicated that two-thirds of the 107 boards around the province agreed "post-secondary education ... should be a prerequisite to becoming a police officer." Research shows that, overall, college-educated officers generate fewer citizen complaints, and are also less likely to use force inappropriately. Among front-line officers who have the most public interactions, having a post-secondary education significantly increases commitment to community policing while promoting a proactive disposition toward working with community members to resolve issues and prevent problems rather than only reacting to calls for service.

As a general rule of thumb, post-secondary education, done properly, increases the capacity for empathy, critical thinking, ethical decision-making, and being receptive to diverse community demographics. One would assume a global perspective and understanding of various cultures, traditions, and norms would be essential given the federal government's immigration targets over the next three years. Education was commonly thought to be the best antidote to ignorance and a vital ingredient of self-awareness. While it is fair to argue that no single cause variable will alter policing completely, the decision to actively signal a willingness to deploy a less educated cadre of police officers is ill-informed.

Given the pace of social and technological change, we are not setting future police officers up for success by removing the prerequisite of post-secondary education. Policing has become more complex over the decades; the premium on transferable skills such as emotional intelligence and cultural competence is more pronounced. High school graduates do not have the necessary knowledge, skills and abilities to compete for jobs with such nuanced requirements. The announcement sounds like a win for job seekers. But it will have a limited impact on hiring practices and adverse outcomes for police and the community downstream.

"Small Act of Kindness" Made Newcomer Feel Welcome in Durham Region

Published by Metroland Media Group - Durham Region: Jun 10, 2023

In an age of polarization and division, it is easy to focus on stories that highlight our differences and encourage tribalism. Yet every now and again, we are reminded of the kindness, compassion and enduring spirit of community that makes Durham Region a beautiful place to live, work and belong.

I had the opportunity to meet a local artist who moved to Canada from Chennai, India, in 2019. Malini relocated to Ontario with her husband, an internationally trained professional who had secured employment in the province. With "permanent residency" status secured, they hoped to forge a new life. She describes herself as a self-taught artist who, despite being an IT professional, was pursuing her passion and creativity. She owns and operates a small art studio where she provides art lessons for children, creates original culturally themed artwork and participates in local cultural events.

Like many immigrants of Indian ancestry, she explored Brampton and Mississauga as options to establish her new life. However, while the allure of common culture made living in the west end a safe choice, Durham's comparatively competitive housing market made them reconsider; they ultimately bought a home in a less diverse community and began the process of social integration.

The first few months brought all the usual challenges experienced by new immigrants: feelings of isolation, struggles with belonging, and all the emotional turmoil that comes from leaving friends, family and culture behind. Integration is often a slow and lonely process. When all the well-meaning advice has been received and the newness and excitement of change wears off, the business of community building and acceptance of new routines begins. It really is the first test of adaptability, resilience and grit required of global citizens.

According to the Durham Immigration and Inclusion Community Plan 2020-2024, the three pillars of community integration are economic prosperity, service co-ordination, and community belonging. The third pillar explicitly commits to making "Newcomers feel welcomed and included in Durham Region, (so they may) ... participate socially, economically and culturally in their community." Malini's story is an exemplar of the purpose of the Durham Immigration and Inclusion Community Plan.

Malini taught just two local students at first. Her business has since grown to include virtual classes with upwards of 25 students. She gives back to the community by facilitating a free online class for children each month. Her business brings Indian cultural art to the community promoting cultural competence in the region.

She has embraced life in Durham, participating in numerous cultural and social events. Clarington Mayor Adrian Foster presented her with the "Excellence Award in Art" for successfully serving the region of Durham. She in turn presented the mayor with one of her original paintings.

One of the most touching parts of Malini's story, however, was her retelling of her experience with a gentle Caucasian man in his 80s, a longtime resident of Durham and her new next-door neighbour. He shared his lawn mower until they purchased their first one and stopped by regularly for driveway conversations. That small act of kindness, the recognition of their humanity regardless of any racial or cultural differences, truly made them feel like a part of the community.

Seeing community engagement and integration in action makes me proud to be a longtime Durham resident. Despite all the tales of polarization and division we hear about, this was truly a celebration of common humanity and belonging in our region.

Learning About Systemic Racism Isn't a Black-and-White Issue for my Brown-and-White Son

Published by CBC First Person: Jun 14, 2023

"Dad, am I a bad person?"

The question made my head whip around to look at my eight-year-old son in the back seat of the car. His school day had just ended and those were the first words he said as he buckled up.

"Why do you ask, raja?" I replied, attempting to sound as nonchalant as possible. I knew something did not feel right. Using the common Indian term of affection was clearly a sign I was retreating to a place of cultural comfort; that's how my parents referred to me growing up.

My son seemed far less perturbed by the question. There is an innocence to children who have not yet been jaded by the nuances of racial discourse. He had simply listened to a lesson, no different than the times tables they practised in the first period.

Ironically, both lessons will probably contribute to his life moving forward. One to multiply his mathematical competence, the other to sharpen his capacity to divide.

Reverberations of 'seismic racism'
As we drove home, my child told me his class had learned about "seismic racism", but he was still confused. Not wanting to shut down the conversation, I asked him what seismic racism was, and he casually filled me in. "It is when all white people are mean to black and brown people because that is how the world works," he replied confidently.

"Do you mean systemic racism?" I asked just to clarify. "Maybe," was the response. "So, Dad, am I a bad person because Mum is white?"

My son is biracial. His mother is white, of British ancestry, a second-generation Canadian. I am a first-generation immigrant of Indian ancestry with some Portuguese DNA, the remnants of 450 years of Portuguese colonization of India.

Early in his life, we didn't explicitly discuss his racial identity. Perhaps we were hopeful that labelling would be a bygone practice, perhaps we wished he'd grow up to see a multi-racial society as simply normal.

Three years after he was born, his mother and I divorced. By the time he was six, I had remarried, and we were now a part of a beautiful, blended family. My wife, of Scottish ancestry whose family had settled in Canada more than 200 years previously, also had mixed-race children from a previous relationship. Our home and our family was truly representative of the Canadian mosaic.

Now, confronted with his question, I bought time and said we'd talk about it after dinner when his step-mum came home.

You would think we were perfectly suited to deal with this situation. After all, we had three children who'd had multiple experiences of some variation of the same thing, from the child-like curiosity behind questions like, "Why do you have green eyes and dark curly hair?" or that seemingly innocuous query that all immigrants encounter way too often, "Where are you really from?" I had dealt with that bias over my 28 years in Canada, but my children simply saw themselves as kids from the neighbourhood.

More complicated than casting blame
Yet here we were again, and once more I shared my angst and fears with my wife. I wondered out loud whether my child, who is half-brown and half-white, was considered half oppressor and half oppressed? Does his white privilege overshadow his brown historical subjugation? Or does his brown historical subjugation overshadow his white privilege? How do I help my child make sense of this polarized world?

As identity politics has made its way into elementary schools, I wonder if anyone has thought about how biracial children perceive these simplistic and reductive labels. And above all, I'm deeply aware that we racialized parents must teach our biracial kids how to navigate a world that is still sorting them based on their skin-deep characteristics.

In the end, we explained that while some people feel it is important to assign blame and create shame, history is more complicated than that.

We told him that his identity cannot be separated neatly into little colour bundles. He is a combination of his history, his experiences and his choices. We told him he is a person first and a person of colour second. We told him character matters more than skin colour. All these things we told him were things we'd said before to our older kids.

He looked me square in the face. "So, I'm not half-bad then? Why didn't you just say that in the car?"

Then he asked, "Can I go play on my iPad for a bit?" My wife and I looked at each other and then back at him. "Sure, raja," I said. As I glanced back at my wife, I knew this would not be the last time we would have this conversation at home.

Durham Columnist on What Fathers Have in Common

Published by Metroland Media Group - Durham Region: Jul 8, 2023

You need to know me to like me; you need to like me to trust me; you need to trust me to not see me as an "other" — that is a modified and paraphrased version of an old business saying, and yet sage advice for anyone who feels like their local social demographics are rapidly changing.

For the record, that "feeling" is completely supported by the facts. According to Statistics Canada, Durham Region's population has increased significantly since 2016. All the municipalities in Durham (except Scugog) experienced population growth; Clarington experienced the highest rate of growth, followed by Oshawa and then Pickering. But what if you have more in common with your new neighbours than you realize?

Since we recently celebrated Father's Day, I thought I would highlight a very special example of our common humanity: the shared values of fathers everywhere. Meet Harry, a first-generation Canadian of Indian ancestry. He moved with his family to Canada in 1995 and chose Durham Region to call home. His family has lived here ever since. Harry and his wife, Sylvia, typify many of the norms assigned to people born shortly after the Second World War. They prioritize the nuclear family, believe in hard work, and attend church service every Sunday without fail. They see adversity as a normal feature of life, something to be overcome by resilience and grit.

Harry has always prided himself on being self-made. Like many men in the golden age of life, he will regale you with stories of yesteryear any chance he gets. He loves to sing and does a mean impression of "Delilah" by Tom Jones — also, like many other older adult citizens, he has seen Jones perform at Casino Rama.

Being the entrepreneur that he is, Harry bought a sandwich shop, Submarine Fair, in the Whitby Mall shortly after arriving in Canada. Alongside his wife, they worked six days a week, 12 hours each day. Years later, he owned and operated a dry-cleaning business in Ajax, a business he worked at for more than a decade, which would shutter under the weight of the COVID-19 pandemic. Yet, if you ask him today, he will still tell you that it is always better to work for yourself than some corporate interest.

If you asked them why they worked as hard as they did, they would tell you it was so that their children could have a better future. Turns out their hard work paid off: one of their sons now runs his own business and the other is a college professor. Their immigrant journey was selfless, largely determined by the benefits their children and grandchildren would enjoy.

Now pause for just one moment, play that story back, then ask yourself: couldn't that have been any Tom, Dick or Harry you may already know, rather than an immigrant who moved to Canada? Yet, that story was about one particular Harry, my father, a first-generation Canadian. An older adult citizen who sits in front of the television beside my mother, Sylvia, to whom he has been married for almost 50 years, cheering for any sports team with the word "Toronto" in its name. I'm not sure what it is about immigrants, but we tend to be very patriotic about the country we get to call home and a little over the top about sports!

Couldn't this have been a story about your father? Perhaps we are not that different after all.

From Odesa to Oshawa: The Journey of a Ukrainian Tattoo Artist

Published by Metroland Media Group - Durham Region: Jul 29, 2023

"I stood 100 metres from the border crossing; that was my home, but I knew I could never go back."

He waited with bated breath for his son to make the crossing safely. The moments passed slowly, and a flurry of thoughts flashed through his mind.

Maskym was born in the small village of Old Shompoly, not far from Odesa in Ukraine. The son of a grocer would find himself in downtown Whitby after the Russian invasion.

One day, while standing in front of a class, when asked to introduce himself and share his goals, he found himself giving voice to an inner dream that he had never vocalized previously: "I'm Maskym Fedorenko, and I want to be a tattoo artist."

I met Max, as he refers to himself now, at Headrush Tattoos at 215 Dundas St. E. in downtown Whitby. Over the duration of my three-hour sitting, Max and I chatted about his life in Ukraine, the war that made home unsafe, and the journey that ultimately brought him to Durham Region. Max and his family were granted a visa for Canada as part of the Canada-Ukraine Authorization for Emergency Travel (CUAET) measures, implemented following the Russian invasion. The CUAET allows Ukrainian nationals to stay in Canada for up to three years. Along with his wife, Veronica, and son, Roman, Max now lives in Oshawa and works in Whitby.

When Russia invaded Ukraine, Max was out of the country working in Germany. His passion for art and tattoos took him to Bavaria, where he worked with experienced tattoo artists to hone his craft and master his trade. His son was with family back home in Ukraine when the invasion began; Max knew he had to get his son to safety.

The story about the fears he experienced at the Ukrainian border waiting for his son was one of many he shared with me over our three hours together. I saw in him a sense of loss for his home in Ukraine, but also hope for a new life in Durham. The fact that Canada has the largest Ukrainian diaspora in the world helps with community integration and transition, but starting over is always a challenge.

They have been in Canada for three months now, trying to start their life over. Veronica teaches dance in Toronto and their son is adjusting to life in Ontario. Max, meanwhile, is sharing his talent and working hard to build his reputation with the Durham community. When I asked what he liked best about his job, he replied, "I get happy by being able to transform my client's ideas into reality and watch them smile."

He drew the tattoo freehand, directly on my arm — a lost art, uncommon nowadays — many tattoo shops primarily use a stencil and merely trace over. Max proceeded to do some of the best work I've ever had — but more than his artistic talent, I appreciated the conversation with this young man. I smiled as I listened to his story, witnessed his creativity, and found commonality with a fellow traveller.

These little conversations I have with people around town only serve to reinforce the beauty of diversity in our region. Our postal codes make us neighbours, but our common humanity transforms us into a community.

One more reason that makes Durham Region a great place to live, work, play, and do business.

It's Not All About the Money for Durham's Immigrants

Published by Metroland Media Group - Durham Region:
Sep 2, 2023

A better life in Canada does not just mean a better job. For some new immigrants the motivation has nothing to do with employment. Anisha and Rohan, a newly married couple in their mid-30s, moved from their home in Bengaluru (formerly Bangalore — the Silicon Valley of India) to Whitby.

They both possess advanced degrees in biotechnology and business, respectively, and each brings more than a decade of work experience with them.

They explained that they came to Canada to get away from the rat-race back home. They had great jobs, a promising life and yet wanted something more. They appreciated the natural beauty of Canada, the quality of life available, and many simple things that many Canadians take for granted every day.

Much of our social and political discourse on Canadian immigration policy focuses almost exclusively on economic objectives. Undoubtedly, economic metrics are central to our evaluation. Immigration policy is not wholly altruistic, as some would like to pretend. According to the Council on Foreign Relations, "Canada admits new permanent residents under four main categories. In 2021, 62 per cent of immigrants were admitted through economic pathways, 20 per cent through family sponsorship, 15 per cent as protected persons and refugees, and three per cent for humanitarian or other reasons." There is an instrumental function to all government policy, pretending otherwise does not change the reality. But pragmatic function does not automatically devalue purpose.

Canada has a declining birth rate. For a population to sustain itself, it requires a birth rate of 2.1 per woman;

our Canadian birth rate in 2023 is around 1.4 per woman, which means that without immigration, we cannot replenish our own population.

Canada has an aging population. Currently, it takes tax revenue from approximately four working-age adults to pay for each retiree. Immigration policy is intended to address that ratio, which will bolster service capability for retirement-aged citizens.

Finally, immigration seeks to address labour-market shortages by bringing in highly skilled and educated workers. Most new immigrants arrive through the economic category, which means they are here with functional purpose deemed necessary for the betterment of the Canadian economy.

Yet for Anisha and Rohan, gainful employment, while valuable, was not the only determinant of a better life. They describe themselves as "foodies," who enjoy sampling various cuisines available at the increasingly diverse restaurant options in Durham. They love hiking the local trails, and even ventured out and tried skiing.

"The stereotype is real; Canadians are truly friendly," said Anisha, when recalling how helpful the local transit drivers were when they first arrived and didn't know their way around. Rohan explained that life back home was highly transactional, fast paced and impersonal. Durham feels a little more like home to them every day; they love being a part of the culture here and are glad they made the leap to start life anew.

Debating immigration policy is completely within bounds for a democratic society, but it may help to remember that behind every statistic is a real person, family, and life, waiting to become a part of the Canadian mosaic. Turns out there is more to life than money after all.

Gerard Keledjian: Grit and Resilience Turns Hope to Reality

Published by Metroland Media Group - Durham Region:
Oct 15, 2023

"Life in Canada sometimes feels like a board game. For new immigrants, just learning the rules can be a challenge that prevents them from playing," said Gerard Keledjian.

The Pickering resident shared his early experiences as a new immigrant. His story, like so many others trying to forge a new beginning, was filled with struggle, disappointment, doubt and fear. But resilience and perseverance allowed Keledjian to parlay those early lessons into a successful life and business in the media communication sector.

Today, Keledjian is the founder and managing director of New Canadians TV network (a division of New Horizons Media Inc.), a social enterprise organization that employs a diverse team of internationally trained media professionals. Their flagship national TV show has been airing weekly on OMNI Television since 2015.

New Canadians is the only immigrant-focused television program in Canada featuring "immigrant success stories, news, resources for pre-arrival preparation and settlement" as well as insights on employment, entrepreneurship and skills training, easing new immigrant integration into the workforce and Canadian society.

This November, they begin their ninth season, an accomplishment of significance for anyone in the media and communication industry, but particularly sweet for someone who began his media journey in Canada as a volunteer at a local community TV channel because his international education and experience was undervalued.

His journey to Canada followed an eight-year stay in Dubai, United Arab Emirates, where he worked in broadcast news as an executive producer for a large multinational news network.

By the time he moved to Canada, he had more than 13 years' experience at a senior level within the news industry. He believed his education and experience would be readily transferable to productive employment in Toronto, but it took several years and a great deal of grit to make his dreams a reality. Here the lived experience of new immigrants rarely matches the glib rhetoric often espoused about valuing the economic contributions of diverse newcomers.

Finding himself at the intersection of media and immigration, he eventually carved out his own niche. Motivated by a sense of social responsibility, Keledjian was determined to help other new immigrants, especially media professionals, learn the rules of the Canadian labour market "board game."

In slightly more than a decade in Ontario, Keledjian established a professional immigrant network for media professionals through TRIEC (Toronto Region Immigrant Employment Council); he works with non-profits helping them develop cost-effective content solutions while recognizing their financial constraints.

A proud Durham resident himself, he gives back to the community through his commitment to developing the next generation of media professionals in Durham region. His company hires student interns from the broadcasting — radio and contemporary media program in the faculty of media, art and design at Durham College in Oshawa, a partnership that has been in place since 2017.

When I asked Keledjian what he is most proud of, he looked like he was cycling past the memories of his last 13 years here, then simply stated he was grateful to find his place in Canada, his work in Toronto that allows him to make a living, his home in Durham and the opportunity to make a positive impact in the lives of others. Now that is taking hard lessons and positively paying it forward.

Proposed Legislation Would Remove a Barrier for Immigrants

Published by Metroland Media Group - Durham Region: Dec 5, 2023

"When newcomers to Ontario get a meaningful chance to contribute, everyone wins."
– David Piccini, Ontario Minister of Labour, Immigration, Training and Skills Development

"Is this performative or will it actually stop discrimination in the job market?" That was a question I was asked at the end of a guest speaking engagement where I mentioned the proposed new legislation by the Ontario government that would ban the use of "Canadian work experience" as a requirement in job postings or application forms.

I presented to a group of internationally educated professionals seeking employment in their field of expertise. I was asked to share my thoughts on new immigrant integration and potential barriers to full employment.

As an immigrant myself, it is heart-wrenching to hear questions like the one I was asked. It reveals the fears and trepidations many highly educated immigrant professionals face when embarking on a job hunt. The tone of voice and the sombre expression on the face of the person asking the question revealed a level of angst often underappreciated.

Whether the proposed legislation will have the desired impact its advocates purport will depend on the attitudes of employers and the biases of recruiters. It will require a shift in the way we think about knowledge and experience. In a global society where labour moves relatively seamlessly around the planet, the physical location where experience is acquired is less relevant than the transferable utility those skills and knowledge bring to the Canadian workforce.

In the first nine months of 2023, more than 162,000 new immigrants arrived in Ontario. According to the most recently published census data, "immigrants (including non-permanent residents) comprised approximately 28 per cent of Durham's population." By comparison to other GTA regions, Durham has the lowest percentage of immigrants.

In Canada, immigrants admitted under the economic category are selected based on their capacity to contribute to the economy and meet labour market demands, or to create economic opportunities through self-employment. The economic category is one of the primary categories for immigrant selection, accounting for more than half of new immigrants to Canada.

Yet many new immigrants, including those arriving under the economic category, find themselves woefully underemployed. Piccini said in an early November 2023 statement, "For far too long, too many people arriving in Canada have been funnelled toward dead-end jobs they're overqualified for. We need to ensure these people can land well-paying and rewarding careers that help tackle the labour shortage."

The Ontario government plans to introduce legislation that, if passed, would ban the use of "Canadian work experience" as a requirement in job postings or application forms. The intention is to allow new immigrants a pathway into employment that matches their qualifications. If passed, this new legislation will mean "Ontario would be the first in Canada to include provisions on Canadian experience in employment standards legislation."

Whether this proposed legislation is performative, or substantive will depend on our collective ability to get out of our own way. It will be contingent on our capacity to see value in plurality and demonstrate a willingness to embrace a multitude of perspectives.

A changing social context can be the catalyst for economic growth, creativity and the emergence of new opportunities — or we can choose to believe that the best measure of experience is its acquisition within a defined area contained within an imaginary line on a map.

Locally Focused, Diverse Perspectives Matter Greatly for Regional Politics

Published by Metroland Media Group - Durham Region: Feb 17, 2024

My local riding of Durham Region is heading to the ballot box.

According to a communication from the Prime Minister's office, a by-election will be held on March 4, 2024, in the electoral district of Durham.

After 10 years as the Member of Parliament for the Durham Riding, former Conservative Party leader Erin O'Toole resigned and vacated his seat. It opened the door to the upcoming by-election that will bring new representation to Ottawa.

Canadian federal politics routinely overshadows provincial and municipal elections; this focus on the national over the local may be a contributing factor to steadily declining voter turnout across Ontario.

Closer to home, Oshawa saw its lowest-ever voter turnout for a municipal election in 2022, with just 18.4 per cent of eligible voters casting a ballot. That is a troubling statistic, given that local politics has a more direct and immediate impact on our daily lives, our community, and our local economy than most things coming out of Ottawa.

A Little Durham Region, Ontario History

A Conservative candidate has consistently held the federal seat in Durham since 2004. In fact, dating back to 1904, when the electoral district was first contested, the Conservatives have faired significantly better than the Liberals in this riding. Since its inception, Durham has been represented by the Conservative Party for 84 of 119 years.

That said, the next Conservative candidate would be ill-advised to consider the riding a lock and should be prepared to appeal to an ever-shifting population demographic in the region. Likewise, left-leaning candidates would benefit from recognizing the diversity of viewpoints that exist within minority populations.

The region is growing with a healthy demographic mix. Approximately 47 per cent of Durham's immigrant population arrived in Canada under the economic admissions category, while a further 35 per cent were sponsored by family.

Both factors bode well for the future, as Durham welcomes people with the capacity to contribute to economic prosperity while being rooted in family and community.

Appealing to the new voters in the region will be essential to securing their support. The riding of Milton may offer an essential lesson in electoral unpredictability.

A Lesson from Milton, Ontario
A federal redistribution took effect for Milton by the 2015 election, which the Conservative Party won, but they have lost every subsequent election thereafter.

In 2015, Lisa Raitt of the Conservative Party won the riding with 22,378 votes. In 2019, she secured an almost identical number of votes and still lost the riding by almost 9,000 votes to the Liberal Party candidate, Adam Van Koeverden.

In the space of four years, the number of eligible voters in Milton increased by 13,000. If Raitt secured the same voters she had in the previous election, it suggests that the Conservative Party was unable to grow its base in that riding.

The failure to appeal to Milton's newest residents arguably cost the Conservative Party a federal seat — one they are yet to recover given Van Koeverden retained his seat in 2021 with an even larger margin over the next Conservative Party candidate, Nadeem Akbar.

The riding of Durham will experience a federal redistribution this year, with new boundaries and a new name. According to the 2021 Census, the population of Durham Region has increased significantly since 2016.

All the municipalities in Durham (except Scugog) experienced population growth. The region's growth outpaced the neighbouring regions of York, Toronto, and Peel. More than 70 per cent of Durham Region's population growth was through immigration. The similarities make Milton a relevant case study for that reason.

Unity Over Division
When representing a diverse constituency, candidates do not need to pick between appealing to one demographic over another; instead, they should focus on a politics of unity rather than division.

Regardless of what the politicians do within their campaigns, the process only truly works for all citizens when we exercise our civic responsibilities and engage in the democratic process.

Local politics and elections matter. We may want to ensure we don't have another record-breaking low voter turnout cycle; after all, this is our community, where we live, work and play.

Acknowledgements

"I'm Not Your Token: Unapologetic Clarity in Divided Times", was not a book I originally planned to write. I only began my journey as an amateur writer in June of 2023. I drew on my experiences as a professor and an advocate, and decided I wanted to take a bold stand against tokenism and the dangers of simplifying complex social issues into digestible narratives.

It all began with the launch of a Substack publication that I co-founded with my dear friend Brian Sankarsingh. We knew we wanted to provide an unflinching exploration of identity, race, and social dynamics in a world that is increasingly divided. We named our publication Seeking Veritas. - A year and a half later we published over 330 articles spanning 80+ consecutive weeks and ended 2024 among the top 3% of all publishers on the Substack App.

The articles I wrote were a call for honest, unapologetic conversations about inclusion in today's society. They were informed by my longstanding belief that the most powerful way to combat division is through clarity, courage, and open communication. Those articles written over eighteen months became this book you are presently holding in your hand. - But I could not have done it alone.

I must acknowledge Brian Sankarsingh for the unwavering support and camaraderie he has consistently offered me. He has become like an older brother to me and I'm eternally grateful that he wrote the introduction and the section summaries for this book. I also thank Susan Knight who edited my early drafts and helped me organize my numerous Substack articles into the coherent sections you found presented within the pages of this book. She has always shared her time with me generously and for that I will always be grateful. And, I would be remiss to not acknowledge my ex-wife and still dear friend Kristen. She encouraged me to pick up the pen in the first place, and many of the ideas I ultimately wrote about were first discussions we had over wine and scotch at the end of a long day. While our futures are no longer entwined, I will always be grateful that our paths once crossed.

Most importantly, I gathered everything I wrote to date and created this book as a keepsake for my children. I hope it serves to inspire them to never be afraid to think differently and speak openly. I hope it motivates them to follow the path of the unsafe independent thinkers, whose ideas are always exposed to the dangers of controversy, but who in the end fear less the label of dissenter than the comfort of conformity.